Cordon Bleu

# Dictionary of Cookery Terms

Cordon Bleu

# Dictionary of
# Cookery Terms

Macdonald and Jane's
London

Published by
Macdonald and Jane's Publishers Ltd
Paulton House
8 Shepherdess Walk
London N1

This impression 1977


Designed by Melvin Kyte
Printed by Waterlow (Dunstable) Ltd

These recipes have been adapted from the Cordon Bleu Cookery Course
published by Purnell in association with the London Cordon Bleu
Cookery School
Principal : Rosemary Hume ; Co-Principal : Muriel Downes
Quantities given are for 4 servings.
Spoon measures are level unless otherwise stated.

# Contents

# Introduction

A cook in the true Cordon Bleu tradition will always enjoy her time spent in the kitchen. This type of pleasure comes of course partly from seeing the final result presented as a tasty dish on the table, but also to a large extent from the exercise of knowledge and skill in cooking. A Cordon Bleu cook will know not only *what* the recipe books recommend, but why; she will know what foods will combine well and she will know how to make the best use of the materials and time available. Throughout this series we have tried to provide this type of information, in the course of detailing our recipes.

Now, in this Cordon Bleu Dictionary of Cookery Terms, we hope to cover the ground more thoroughly. Here, in a single small volume, is a handbook that can serve as a reference whatever you are doing in the kitchen. We have included foods both strange and familar, technical cookery terms for the methods we use, terms for cooking implements and all kinds of fascinating information. If you really enjoy food you will probably enjoy simply leafing through the pages, reading for the pleasure of discovery.

Do you know that there are two types of almond, one of which is poisonous? Do you know what zakouska is? You probably have lots of small jars in your kitchen, full of herbs and spices; but would you recognise the herbs if you saw them growing, and do you know from which countries and plants the spices come? Maybe you can get along without this information, but any housewife needs to know the different cuts of meat and how they are best prepared.

There are no recipes in this book, but nevertheless it could serve as a standby for new cooks and more experienced hostesses. It is packed with information, all of which is based on the cookery methods taught in the Cordon Bleu School. Absorb even half of what is here and you will be a mine of information to your gourmet friends.

Rosemary Hume
Muriel Downes

## Agar-agar

A setting agent prepared from seaweed and used in jellies and cold soufflés, when animal extracts like gelatine are prohibited (eg. in a vegetarian diet). Also used pharmaceutically.

## Aigrette

A batter savoury, the best known being cheese and anchovy. Cheese aigrettes are choux pastry with cheese added, dropped into deep fat in small quantities to cook until golden-brown and well puffed. Fillets of anchovy are dipped in fritter batter and deep fried to become anchovy aigrettes.

## Aioli

A mayonnaise from the Provence region of France, in which a few cloves of crushed garlic are blended with the egg yolks before the olive oil is worked in and the mixture sharpened with lemon juice or vinegar. Served with boiled fish, boiled vegetables, shellfish, cold meats.

## Allspice

(or **Jamaican pepper**)
(*Pimenta officinalis*)
The seed of the Jamaican pepper, called allspice because its flavour resembles a mixture of cinnamon, cloves and nutmeg. (It is NOT a mixed spice.) May be ground in a mill like peppercorns; used for flavouring meat dishes, particularly grills.

## Allumettes

Matchstick-shaped pieces of fried potato, *pommes allumettes*. Also the name given to a French pâtisserie of fingers of puff pastry spread with royal icing.

## Almond

Kernel of the nut of the almond tree of which there are two varieties, sweet and bitter. Sweet almonds are more commonly used. Occasionally a small proportion of bitter almonds (about 2 per cent) is included in a mixture for flavouring; a larger proportion is poisonous. Best known types are Jordan and Valencia, both from Spain: the former is longer, finer and more expensive and mainly used for dessert while the latter, broad and flat, is used for marzipan and in cakes.

## Aluminium foil

Aluminium rolled into a sheet in standard or heavy thicknesses, both excellent for sealing food from the air, or from direct heat, in refrigeration or cooking.

## Amyli

see **Tamarind**

## Anchovy

Small Mediterranean fish with a distinctive flavour, usually imported into Britain as fillets preserved in brine or oil. Used in salads and savouries, while essence from the fish is used in flavouring savoury butters, sauces and devils. Excess salt is removed from anchovies by soaking in milk.

# Angel cake
A delicate textured white cake baked in a special circular mould with a funnelled base, from a mixture of egg whites, sugar and fine flour. Originally American.

# Angelica
(*Archangelica officinalis*)
A herb which grows as a tall, handsome plant with a pleasant flavour. The stalks are candied, chopped and mixed with dried fruit, or cut into fancy shapes for decorating cakes and sweets.

# Angels on horseback
Oysters rolled in thin rashers of bacon and grilled or baked until crisp, then served on buttered toast. A well-known savoury.

# Angler fish
Caught off the French coast for bouillabaisse; not well-known in England.

# Aniseed
Pungent oil extracted from the herb anise (*Pimpinella anisum*), used for flavouring sweets and apéritifs.

# Apple
There are two main types of this fruit: dessert (for eating) and cooking, the latter being sharply acid, making them pulpy and soft when cooked. Sweet dessert apples become tough and leathery when cooked, though some acid-flavoured pippins cook well. The commonest cooking apples are the *Bramley's Seedling* and *Lane's Prince Albert*, the former being re-garded as the best. It is medium to large, greenish-yellow in colour and cooks with a sharp, pleasant flavour and a fluffy pulp. In season from November to April. Prince Albert is the next best, in season at the same time. It has a juicy, white flesh and a bright green shiny skin.

**Dessert apples:**
*Cox's Orange Pippin* Probably the best of the dessert apples, certainly the best known; has pips which rattle when the ripe apple is shaken. Crisp, creamy yellow and aromatic flesh, with skin greenish-yellow on one side and a red flush on the other; medium to small. In season November to late January.
*Worcester Pearmain* Medium sized, conical-shaped with a deep eye. The skin is greenish-yellow in colour on one side and bright crimson on the other; the flesh is crisp and white. In season from beginning of September to end of October.
*Beauty of Bath* Small apple with yellow skin, heavily streaked with red; round and slightly flat in shape; pink-tinged white flesh. Ripens in August but does not keep.
*Blenheim Orange* Large, round fruit with crisp, yellow nut-flavoured flesh that is excellent for cooking as well as eating. Skin is dull yellow, with deep red streaks and red flush. In season November and December; mostly found in private gardens because trees only bear well when fully matured.
*Laxton's Superb* and *Laxton's Epicure* Both are a pippin cross, the latter maturing somewhat later than the former. Epicure looks and tastes like a Cox's, Superb is slightly conical and has a yellowish skin with red streaks. In season September to November.

# Apricot

Small, golden-coloured fruit with a velvety skin. Grown in large quantities in Spain and South Africa. Excellent for drying, bottling, compotes, tarts and flans; can be eaten as dessert fruit but the flavour is brought out better by cooking.

# Armagnac
see **Brandy**

# Arrowroot
A very fine starch used as a thickening agent and, with milk, as an invalid or baby food. For thickening clear sauces and fruit syrups, slake arrowroot with a little cold water before adding to the hot liquid. Arrowroot jells on boiling and becomes thinner after boiling for one minute. Comes from rhizomes of maranta, grown mainly in the Caribbean.

# Artichoke
A vegetable of which there are two main but quite distinct types, the globe artichoke (*Cynara scolymus*) and jerusalem artichoke (*Helianthus tuberosus*).

The former is green, a bud from a perennial plant of the thistle family, generally boiled for eating. It is served cold with a dressing of oil and vinegar, or hot with butter. In season in Britain in summer, but imported all the year round.

The jerusalem artichoke is a fleshy white tuber of the sunflower family. Its name comes from *girasole*, Italian for sunflower. It has a delicate flavour and is peeled and roasted or boiled and served in different sauces as a winter vegetable.

# Asparagus
A late spring and early summer vegetable grown in special beds; best served as a separate course with melted butter or hollandaise sauce. The English variety has slender green spikes, is sold in bundles after being cropped close to the ground. In France and Belgium it is whiter, thicker, very tender and with only a faint green on the tips.

# Aspic
A clarified jelly for savoury purposes, made from meat, chicken or fish stock depending on the dish with which it is to be used. Must be well flavoured and seasoned and may be slightly sharpened with wine or a few drops of wine vinegar. Food set in or brushed with aspic keeps its attractive appearance and finish for some hours.

# Attelette (or Hâtelet)
A skewer, usually of silver or plate, found in varying sizes and with varying degrees of ornamentation, formerly used in

11

decoration of cold table dishes such as large whole fish, galantines, glazed hams or poultry.

## Atterau

Hot hors d'oeuvre or savoury made by filling a small skewer with squares of ham, mushroom, liver, chicken or shellfish, coating this with a thick béchamel sauce, dipping in egg and breadcrumbs and frying in deep fat. Should be served very hot.

## Aubergine (or Eggplant)

A purple vegetable of striking appearance, originally Indian but now grown mainly in Israel, Spain and France. Can be cooked and served in many ways.

## Aurore

A sauce or soup with a béchamel base to which some well-reduced, fresh tomato pulp has been added. Served with eggs, white meat or vegetables.

## Avgolemono

Chicken stock made into soup with a thickening of rice and beaten eggs, with lemon juice for flavouring. Greek in origin.

## Avocado pear

A vegetable with dark green, thick skin, a large seed, pale green flesh and bland flavour. Resembles a pear in size and shape but is normally eaten in hors d'oeuvre and salads. Grows freely in warm climates.

## Baba

An individual small cake baked in a dariole mould from the same light yeast mixture as used for a savarin, with the addition of a few currants. Soaked in syrup after baking and, as *baba au rhum,* sprinkled with rum before serving.

## Baclava

A traditional sweet dish from Greece and the Middle East. Very thin layers of pastry are brushed with melted butter and sprinkled with chopped nuts, cut into diamonds or squares and baked. Boiling syrup or honey is poured over them and the baclava are left to cool before serving.

## Bacon

The side or flitch of a pig after it has been cured and after the fore (gammon) and hind (ham) quarters have been removed. May be smoked or unsmoked (green), the latter being particularly good in cooked dishes because it has less saltpetre; sold as collar (from the neck), streaky (from the flank), back (from the loin), or long back.

## Bain marie (au)

To cook at a temperature just below boiling point in a bain marie (a saucepan standing in a larger pan of simmering water). Used in the preparation of sauces, creams and food liable to spoil if cooked over direct heat. May be carried out on top of the stove or in the oven. A double saucepan gives a similar effect. Sauces and other delicate dishes may be kept hot in a bain marie under simmering heat.

## Bake
To cook by means of dry heat in the oven, as in the case of bread or cakes. See also **Roasting.**

## Bakewell tart
An open, shortcrust pastry tart lined with red jam or jelly and filled with an almond cake mixture before being baked.

## Baking powder
A raising agent consisting of one part cream of tartar to two parts bicarbonate of soda, mixed with rice flour or potato starch.

## Baklava
see **Baclava**

## Ballotine
A small bird, or leg of a bird, boned and stuffed ; served sliced or whole according to size. When served cold it is usually coated with a chaudfroid, decorated and glazed in aspic, or if hot with a Madeira sauce and a garnish.

## Balm
A perennial herb with a lemon-scented foliage, a handful of which makes a refreshing tea-like drink when infused in boiling water (see **Tisane**). Also known as lemon balm.

## Bamboo shoots
Used in curries and Chinese cooking ; have a delicate flavour and yellowish-white colour. Imported into Britain only in canned form.

## Banana
A small elongated fruit with yellow skin and soft juicy flesh which, if ripe, is full of flavour. Can be baked in its skin, or peeled and fried in batter for serving with meat or as a dessert but usually eaten raw.

## Banbury cake
A small oval cake of flaky pastry filled with rich mincemeat. Named after the Oxfordshire town where it originated. See also **Eccles Cake.**

## Bannock
Traditional Scottish cake of wheat, barley or oat bread flour raised with yeast or soda. One of the best known, the Selkirk bannock, has sultanas, currants and candied peel in a yeast dough.

## Barbecue
A meal roasted or grilled in the open, usually over charcoal and generally steak, chops, etc. Comes from the French *barbe à queue,* in which a whole ox was roasted on the spit. The modern version is a small gridiron set sold for use in the garden.

## Bass
Salt water fish averaging 3-6 lb weight, round in shape, silvery in appearance ; caught off the southern coasts of England. Fished mainly for sport, but its firm, white flesh does have a good flavour.

## Baste
To spoon hot fat/liquid over food as it roasts to keep it succulent and moist.

## Bâtarde
see **Blanche**

13

## Bath bun

Rich dough with some sultanas and candied peel made into a large bun which traditionally has coarse sugar crystals sprinkled on top. Named after the town of Bath, where it originated.

## Bath chap

Cured and smoked cheek of pig, boiled and finished as ham but usually sold already cooked.

## Batter

An egg, flour and milk mixture for frying or baking. Proportions vary; pancakes, for instance, require a thin batter, whereas a Yorkshire pudding batter must be thick.

## Batterie de cuisine

Expression used in France for essential kitchen equipment such as pots, pans, etc.

## Bavarois

Milk, cream and egg yolks made into a rich custard, flavoured with chocolate, coffee, vanilla etc., and set with gelatine.

## Bay

Used fresh or dried, the leaves of the bay tree (*Laurus nobilis*) have a flavour that goes well in soups, meat dishes and sauces. Used with parsley and thyme in the traditonal bouquet garni.

## Bean

Many kinds of bean are grown, some for use as a green vegetable, some more suited to drying.

*Runner beans* The green pods of the runner bean plant, trained up poles or sticks to a height of about 8 ft are sometimes called 'stick' beans to distinguish them

from field runners, which are of lesser quality and not always as clean. The pods may be as long as 10 in without losing their juicy tenderness when sliced and boiled. Smaller varieties about half the height with pods about half the size are now being grown; all are in season in Britain in July and August.

*French bean* Slim, smooth green pods about 5 in long which grow on a dwarf plant and are in season between mid-June and the end of July. Cooked while young and tender, either whole or snapped in two.

*Flageolet,* or *Lima bean* One type of French bean has a pod filled with small, pale green beans of the haricot type. Shelled and cooked either fresh or after being dried, they are regarded as a delicacy.

*Haricot bean* A small bean which is dried after shelling; usually white, but the Dutch Brown and red Rognon de Coq are common on the Continent. Mostly used canned and in soups and stews.

*Butter bean* Large, floury, white bean, excellent as a vegetable. Sold dried or canned.

*Broad beans* The beans are

grey-green and grow inside the long green pod of the plant; in season in Britain in June and July. The beans are shelled from the pods before cooking and should be young and small, like most summer vegetables. If very large they are improved by removing the grey outerskin when cooked. Tossed with chopped savory and butter, or in a poulette sauce, they are the ideal vegetable to go with boiled bacon.

## Béarnaise

A sauce for steaks, tournedos or fillet of beef. It is a rich, brown butter sauce, finished with chopped tarragon and chervil, prepared like a hollandaise, but thicker and with a sharper taste.

## Béchamel

One of the white *sauces mères* or basic sauces from which other sauces may be made. Named after Louis de Béchamel, Marquis of Nointel and Lord Steward of the household of Louis XIV. Milk is infused with onion and spices before being added to a roux of flour and butter.

## Beef

The best eating beef comes from a bullock or young ox, which nowadays are reared specially for flavour and with an eye to the small, compact joints of meat that are in demand. See diagram in appendix for cuts.

## Beer

An alcoholic beverage fermented from malted barley with hops for flavouring.

## Beestings

Milk from a cow the first time it is milked after calving; it is rich enough to make a baked custard set without eggs.

## Beetroot

A rich, dark red winter vegetable. The round (globe) or tapered roots are cooked for their flesh, but sea kale beet (see **Chard**) and spinach beet (see **Spinach**) are grown for their stems and foliage. Care must be taken to see that the skins of beetroot are not broken before cooking or the red colour may bleed away. A test for cooking is that the skin rubs off easily when the beetroot is cooked.

## Beignet

Originally a fritter, the name is also given to small pieces of choux pastry which puff up and turn a golden-brown when dropped into deep fat and cooked on a rising temperature. May be served sweet or savoury, rolled in caster sugar or Parmesan.

## Benedictine

A liqueur made by Benedictine monks at their monastery at Fécamp, France, from an old and still secret recipe.

## Bercy

The Bercy quarter of Paris is known for its wine cellars, so recipes using wine are often called (à la) Bercy. The traditional Bercy sauce is made of white wine, herbs, shallots and light stock in which the food concerned (veal, fish, sweet-breads, etc) has been poached. A liaison of beurre manié is added before serving.

## Beurre blanc

White butter sauce. White wine and chopped shallot are reduced well over gentle heat and unsalted butter added gradually to produce a sauce of creamy colour and consistency for poached or boiled white fish.

## Beurre manié

A liaision of three parts butter and two parts flour, kneaded together to a paste. When food has been poached or simmered, beurre manié is added gradually to the liquid, which must have cooled well below boiling point. The butter melts, drawing the flour into the liquid, which then is boiled again.

## Beurre noir

Black butter sauce. Butter is cooked to a deep nut brown colour then mixed with reduced vinegar, parsley and chopped capers. For use with poached brains, sweetbreads, fish, etc.

## Beurre noisette

Butter cooked to a deep nut brown colour, with lemon juice, chopped parsley and seasoning added. The sauce is poured over the dish (eg. fish shallow fried in butter) while still foaming.

## Bicarbonate of soda
see **Soda**

## Bigarade

Sauce made with bitter orange (bigarade is the French name for a Seville orange) to go with duck or game. It is made on a demi-glace base with the juice and shredded rind of the orange, together with red wine and red currant jelly.

## Bigarreau
see **Cherry**

## Bilberry

Small, black fruit of a low plant which grows wild on moorland (*Vaccinium myrtillus*), also known as blaeberry, whortle-berry, hurt, etc. Ripens from late June to early August, can be served as compote, made into wine, etc., and has a pleasant but not outstanding flavour.

## Biscotins

The French name given to small biscuits served with ice ceams, etc.

## Biscottes

The French name for a rusk or 'pulled' bread; slices of milk bread baked to a golden-brown and sold in packets.

## Biscuit

A piece of plain, sweet or savoury unleavened bread. Most are rolled thin, many are pricked or cut into fancy shapes before baking. Among the great range of sweet biscuits some have a flavoured cream sandwich fil-ling, some are topped with sugar or chocolate.

## Bisque

A rich shellfish soup. The court bouillon in which the fish (usually lobster or prawn) was cooked is strained, thickened with a roux, cream and a butter made from the pounded cooked fish flesh. The shells, crushed to a powder, are also sometimes added. See also **Velouté**.

# Blackberry

(*Rubus fruticosus*)
A fruit growing wild on hedge-rows or cultivated in the garden, usually picked in September for cooking or jam-making, or for jellies. Often made into purée for fool or sauce after cooking because of the quantity of little hard seeds otherwise present. Extra pectin is required for jams and jellies, usually apple.

# Blackcock

(or **Black game**)
A large, handsome game bird, with flesh that is very similar to grouse, and cooked in the same way. The cock is distinguished by white bars above the wing-tips in shining blue-black plumage and weighs about 3–4 lb; the hen, with reddish-brown plumage, is much smaller. Not a common bird, but increasing in numbers in Scotland. In season only from August 20 to December 10.

# Black currant

A soft fruit, rich in vitamin C, picked from late June to end of July. Like the Blackberry it is puréed for sauces, soufflés or fool, but unlike the blackberry it is rich in pectin for jam-making.

# Black pudding

A large black sausage made from a mixture of finely minced pork fat, onions, herbs and pig's blood, possibly with oatmeal or bread for filling. The skin is of prepared gut and the puddings are boiled, usually with their ends tied together in a circle, for keeping. They are boiled again or fried and sliced before eating. There are various regional recipes for black pudding. See also **White Pudding.**

# Blaeberry

see **Bilberry**

# Blanch

To whiten meats and remove strong tastes from vegetables by bringing to the boil from cold water and draining before further cooking. Green vegetables are put into boiling water and cooked for up to one minute.

# Blanche

A white sauce served with fish, chicken or vegetables; made by pouring boiling water on to a roux, after which it should not be boiled but should have more butter added like hollandaise. Caper, green and mustard sauces are also made from sauce blanche and when egg yolks are added it becomes sauce bâtarde, or mock hollandaise.

# Blancmange

A moulded dessert made from cornflour and usually flavoured. Comes from French *blanc-manger*, meaning something white and edible. Was once a form of almond cream.

# Blanquette

A white stew of lamb, veal, chicken or rabbit with a rich sauce made from the stock in which it was cooked. Milk, cream and sometimes egg yolks are added to the sauce.

# Blette

see **Chard**

# Bleu (au)

To cook trout au bleu, plunge the freshly killed fish into a pan containing court bouillon and poach until the skin has a bluish tinge. Usually served with boiled potatoes and melted butter.

## Blewit

Pleasant smelling, edible fungus of the genus *Tricholoma.* Their delicately flavoured, firm flesh is cooked like a mushroom. There are two varieties in England, the wood blewit (*Tricholoma nudum*) whose violet colour may be found in oak woods in autumn, and the fawn capped, violet gilled *Tricholoma personaltum.*

## Blini

Traditional Russian pancake made to go with caviar; baked from a yeast dough made with plain or buckwheat flour, thickly spread with melted butter or soured cream and served hot.

## Bloater

The famous Great Yarmouth bloater is a herring that has been lightly smoked after being salted in brine and dried by hanging by the gills on wooden rods. Usually grilled whole.

## Boil

To cook in water at 212°F. As the water comes to the boil, it bubbles and will bubble for a minute or two before reaching the required temperature. See also **Simmer.**

## Bombe

see **Mould**

## Bonne femme

The name given to dishes incorporating the classic garnish of onions, bacon and mushrooms, generally cooked in a casserole. Sole bonne femme is covered with a sauce containing white wine and mushrooms and browned under the grill.

## Borage

*(Borago officinalis)*
A cucumber flavoured, aromatic herb used to flavour a fruit or wine cup.

## Bordeaux

The name of the French port of Bordeaux and the surrounding region is generally applied to both white and red wines produced in the area, which are put into distinctive, high-shouldered bottles. In England, red Bordeaux wine is known as claret.

## Bordelaise

Food cooked *à la bordelaise* (Bordeaux style) has been cooked with red wine; a sauce bordelaise contains beef marrow as well as red wine.

## Border

see **Mould**

## Bortsch

A soup made from beef stock, which should be strong and flavoured with beetroot, either thick with other vegetables, or clear like a consommé. Comes from Russia and Poland.

## Bouchée

A bouchée (mouthful) is a puff pastry case like a vol-au-vent, but smaller, $1-2\frac{1}{4}$ in diameter, filled with a savoury mixture of shellfish, chicken, mushrooms

etc., bound with a white or velouté sauce.

# Bouillabaisse
A fish broth speciality of mediterranean France, especially Marseilles. Recipes vary according to the district but always include a number of different kinds of fish, herbs and spices, including saffron, which are cooked slowly together until they are like a stew.

# Bouillon
Meat or vegetable stock.

# Boulangère (à la)
A dish containing potatoes and onions cooked in stock in the oven, either with the main dish or separately. The name comes from the days when housewives took their pies, joints, etc. to the local baker (boulanger) to be cooked in his oven.

# Bouquet garni
Bunch of herbs traditionally made up of two or three stalks of parsley, a sprig of thyme and a bay leaf. If used in liquid that is to be strained they may be tied with string, but otherwise are tied in a piece of muslin for easy removal.

# Bourguignonne
*A la bourguignonne* indicates that the dish has been cooked with red wine, onions and mushrooms in the style of the Burgundy region.

# Brains
Calf's and sheep's brains are among the edible offal.

# Braise
To cook slowly by moist heat. The meat or vegetables are browned quickly in fat or oil and placed with a small amount of liquid in a tightly covered container for long, slow cooking. Suited to cheaper cuts of meat which require slow cooking to make them tender; meat may be cooked on a bed of sweated, sliced vegetables. See also **Mirepoix.** Vegetables should be shaken frequently when being braised.

# Bran
The inner husk of grain, separated in grinding. Bran is removed from white flour but remains as a valuable form of roughage in wholemeal flour.

# Brandade
A classic fish cream from the South of France. Made with salt cod, well soaked before cooking. The flesh is pounded and well moistened with olive oil and strongly flavoured with garlic. When creamy the brandade may be served hot with croûtes of fried bread, or cold as a first course.

# Brandy
A spirit distilled from wine, although there are a few brandies made from grain alcohol. Cognac, made from the white wines of the Charente district of France, is regarded as the best, but that from the vines

19

of nearby Armagnac is also highly regarded. Brandy when distilled is colourless, the colour being taken from the wood of the cask in which it matures, or the colour may be added artificially. See also **Eau-de-vie**.

## Brandy snap, or Ginger snap

Flour, butter, syrup, sugar and ginger baked into a wafer-like, crisp biscuit and rolled into a cylinder or cornet shape when baked, and filled with brandy flavoured whipped cream.

## Brawn

Pig's head, stewed, the meat picked from the bones, chopped and pressed. The meat is served cold, sliced thinly and with a sharp dressing. If no special press is available the brawn can be put into small basins and pressed into shape with a weight.

## Brazil nut

The nut or seed of the tall *Bertholletia excelsa* tree, native to the north of Brazil. There may be as many as 32 nuts in one piece of fruit. The wedge-shape of the nut comes from the fact that there are four divisions in the one round fruit; each nut is very hard-shelled and the kernel, rich in oil, is eaten as a dessert nut.

## Bread

Bread may be (a) leavened or (b) unleavened, eg. oatcakes, water biscuits. Of the former, the two main types are those made with yeast as a raising (leavening) agent for the mixture of flour and water or milk, and those which are leavened with baking powder, or bicarbonate of soda and cream of tartar. The latter is known as soda bread, or baking powder bread, contains sour or butter

milk to give extra lightness, and is often baked on a girdle in big rounds cut into four (called farls), or as scones.

In the case of bread leavened with yeast, the proportion of yeast to flour determines the texture of the finished bread. If the proportion is low, for instance 1 oz of yeast to 4 lb or more of flour, or if the dough is drier and firmer, the texture will be close. An open, spongy loaf like the Continental breads comes from a high proportion of yeast or a wetter dough. Water mixed with the dough gives a crisp crust; if milk is used instead, the fat in it makes the crust soft. French bread is baked under steam, which keeps the crust soft while the inside cooks to a light, open texture; steam is then withdrawn and the crust baked crisp. See also **Bran, Flour, Gluten** and **Yeast**.

## Bread sauce
An English sauce which, if well made, is light, creamy and perfectly suited to go with baked or boiled ham, or roast poultry. Milk is first infused with onion and cloves, then breadcrumbs and seasoning are added and the whole is re-heated until boiling. Finally butter is beaten in a small piece at a time.

## Bream
Small to medium-sized round fish. Fresh water bream are found in large ponds and slow-running rivers; their flavour is not very good. Sea bream have large scales and pink-tinged skin, with coarse flesh and again the flavour is poor. Bream are best stuffed and baked, or poached and served with a piquant sauce.

## Bretonne (à la)
Roast or braised mutton, accompanied by haricot beans cooked separately, possibly as a purée.

## Bretonne
A thick velouté sauce to which shredded carrots, celery, onions and leeks cooked in butter have been added; served with fish and eggs.

## Brie
A large, round, flat cheese with a white crust, which takes its name from the district near Paris where it originated. Should be bought and eaten at the peak of ripeness; it is better to buy it cut from the whole cheese, when its condition can be verified, than in small wrapped or boxed portions.

## Brill
Medium to large flat fish, with pale brown skin and firm, creamy coloured flesh. Weighs 2–6 lb and is at its best between September and May; can be cooked like sole or turbot and should be served with a good sauce and garnishes.

## Brine
Salt and water in a strong solution for preserving meats, fish and vegetables.

## Brioche
Very light dough made with yeast, baked as a loaf or as small or medium-sized buns in fluted tins. These traditionally are shaped like cottage loaves and have nut-brown tops. May also be cooked like doughnuts in deep fat.

## Brisling
Young, small herring, usually

sold tinned or cured in England.
See also **Sprat.**

## Broccoli
Vegetable not unlike cauliflower. Purple-sprouting broccoli has a handsome head the size of a small cauliflower, and a flavour which is excellent although not as delicate as cauliflower. With hollandaise sauce it makes a good starter or entremets. Available September and early October. Italian broccoli (calabrese) is in season in July and early August. The side shoots may be trimmed, tied in bundles and cooked like asparagus.

## Broche (en)
Cooked on the spit.

## Brochette
Metal or wood skewer for grilling pieces of meat. See **Kebab.**

## Broiler
see **Chicken**

## Broiling
see **Grilling**

## Brown sauce
A sauce made by cooking a mirepoix in butter, then making a roux with flour and finishing the sauce as for a demi-glace, with the addition of stock; if the stock is not the best, butter may be added to get a better colour.

## Brunoise
A garnish for soups, etc., made by cooking a finely diced mirepoix of vegetables in a small quantity of butter.

## Brussels sprouts
A winter vegetable resembling a miniature cabbage, a member of the *Brassica* family to which cabbages belong. They are best picked after the first frosts of the winter and should be cooked and eaten while still tight and small.

## Bubble and squeak
For using up cooked beef and cabbage leftovers: the beef is sliced and fried and arranged round the cabbage, which is also chopped and fried.

## Buckling
A herring that has been smoked whole; eaten as an hors d'oeuvre without further cooking, with accompaniment of dill cucumber and onion salad.

## Buckwheat
A cereal obtained from the *Fagopyrum esculentum* plant. It is ground into a flour to make pancakes or crumpets in the United States and blinis in Russia, but not much used in England.

## Buffet

A meal in which guests app-roach and help themselves or are served from various dishes laid out on a long table or side-board. The dishes are usually cold, chosen for colour and variety as well as taste, and not only include fish, meat, poultry and salads, but also cold des-serts. Sometimes hot dishes are included.

## Bullace

A small plum rarely seen nowa-days except in the country; greenish-yellow in colour, very sour and about the size of a sloe; makes good jam or fruit cheese.

## Bun

A light yeast dough formed into small shapes, proved and baked. May be made with or without the addition of dried fruit. The tops are glazed before they are taken from the oven.

## Burgundy

The name of the region, and the red and white wines it produces, centred on Beaune. The majority of the wines come from the Côte d'Or region, although Upper and Lower Burgundy also make a considerable con-tribution.

## Butter

The fat produced when ripened cream is churned under certain conditions of temperature, the globules of fat from the milk and cream being broken down and massed into butter. It is the finest fat for cooking and is best used unsalted for this purpose; for other uses it may be salted to taste. *Clarified butter* is that which has been heated and strained to rid it of any extra-neous substances except the fat. This makes the ideal frying medium. See also **Clarify**. *Buttermilk* is what remains after the butter has solidified during churning. It is ideal for soda bread and scones and has a pleasantly sharp taste due to acidity set up in the process.

## Butter cream

A filling or coating for pâtisseries or gâteaux. The three main types have these bases: (a) yolk and syrup, (b) custard and (c) a *meringue cuite* base (see **Mer-ingue**). They are made into a rich, soft mixture with the addition of unsalted butter that has been well creamed and a flavouring like coffee or choco-late, or a fruit purée.

## Butter icing
see **Icing**

## Buttermilk
see **Butter**

23

## Cabbage

A vegetable of the *Brassica* family, like cauliflowers, kale and broccoli; one of the most popular vegetables, with a number of varieties available at different times of the year and some more suited to certain dishes than others.

The varieties are:
SPRING CABBAGE As its name suggests, available from May for several months, and like many other spring vegetables, it is tender. It is smallish and may be distinguished by its oval, pointed heart with its brilliant, delicate green colour and the darker, almost blue-green, outer leaves. It is best plain-boiled in quarters and finished in butter with a sprinkling of herbs, particularly chopped parsley.
WINTER CABBAGES These are available after September. The main types are:
*Green cabbage* Usually about 2 lb in weight, round, with a firm heart; slightly different types maintain a continuity for all purposes from September until February.
*Savoy cabbage* In season from December onwards. Bright green with very crinkly leaves, the outside of which may be browned by frost without the heart being affected. Equally good boiled, with white sauce, or braised, with rolled bacon.
*White Dutch* (also called *Drumhead*) Large, white and hardhearted, making them equally good for shredding in salads or cooking in a little wine or stock.

*Red cabbage* Should be shredded and blanched before cooking (colour can be restored by sprinkling a couple of tablespoons of vinegar with a little sugar over it before cooking). Is served with pork, hare, game and other rich foods. Needs more cooking than the drumhead variety, about one to two hours in a tightly covered pan with $\frac{1}{4}$ pint of stock. May also be cooked with apple and is ideal as salad or winter pickle.

## Cabbage lettuce
see **Lettuce**

## Cabinet pudding
A once-popular hot pudding of breadcrumbs and currants baked in custard with a lemon or vanilla flavouring.

## Caerphilly
A white, mild-flavoured cheese with a close, firm texture, best eaten when freshly cut. Originally Welsh, now made in the western counties.

## Cake
Basically cake is a mixture of flour, fat, sugar and eggs baked in the oven. It may be enriched with fruit or with various flavourings, and is served at tea time or as a dessert.

## Calabrese
see **Broccoli**

## Calf
see **Veal**

## Camembert

A round cheese weighing about 12 oz, pale yellow and smooth-textured with an orange-yellow crust; when ripe it should be soft but not running. Takes its name from the village in the Orne department where a farmer's wife, Madame Harel, is said to have invented it.

## Camomile

(or **Chamomile**)
Heads of the *Anthemis nobilis* plant which, when dried, are used for infusions. See **Tisane**.

## Canapé

A small quantity of savoury mixture piled on to a savoury biscuit, pastry or piece of toasted or fried bread. Lends itself to many forms of decoration to make it eye-catching as well as tasty.

## Candied peel

The pith and peel of citrus fruits, generally lemon, orange and citron, which have been candied by boiling and treating with syrup, then drying. Mainly used in puddings and cakes with dried fruit. Usually bought in the shops, but may be made thus: Cut fruit in half, remove flesh, boil peel gently in water until tender, then drain; cover with strong syrup and leave until semi-transparent. Drain again and dry in gentle heat. Or peel may be put into a thinner syrup (see **Syrup**) at the beginning and simmered gently until syrup is thick and peel translucent, thus shortening the process.

## Candy

A confection that is granulated or grained. Sugar syrup is boiled to 250°F and then gently stirred round the sides of the pan only. The syrup starts to cloud and become thick and stirring continues until it is all grained. Flavouring is added and the candy is turned out to cool on to a surface that must be both warm and oiled.

## Cannelloni

A large tube-shaped Italian pasta. The tubes are partly boiled, then stuffed with a meat or cheese filling and generally covered with a sauce in which cooking is completed. Sometimes thin pancakes, rolled and stuffed and coated with cream or cheese sauce, are used instead of the pasta.

## Cape gooseberry

*(Physalis)*
A round yellow berry that grows inside a calyx similar to the Japanese lantern plant, imported from the Cape area of South Africa, mostly canned or as jam, but fresh around Christmas. Fresh cape gooseberries may be served as dessert, or dipped in fondant after calyx is turned back and eaten as a sweetmeat.

## Caper

The bud of the *Capparis spinosa* plant which grows in Spain, France and Italy. The smaller the

25

bud the more delicate the flavour. Capers are mainly used for flavouring sauces. Nasturtium seeds soaked in brine then pickled are sometimes used as substitutes.

## Capercailzie

A large game bird (7–10 lb) of the grouse family, now quite rare, but once plentiful in Scottish highlands and moors; hang for 10 days and roast.

## Capon

A young cockerel treated by injection then specially fattened for the table; has delicate white flesh, weighs 5–8 lb, ideal for large family meals. May be stuffed and roasted like turkey, and served hot or cold. Alternatively, for serving cold poach whole bird, remove and slice suprêmes, and coat with chaud-froid sauce. If bird is roasted, aspic jelly alone may be used.

## Capsicum

The name covers the whole range of peppers and chillies, from the large green or red peppers, also known as bell peppers or pimientos, which are mild and sweet, to the tiny hot chillies found mainly as flavouring in pickles and chutneys. Dried and ground these hot chillies become chilli powder or cayenne pepper. The big peppers are more easily digested if blanched before use. They may be bought fresh or canned. Paprika comes from the big red pepper, dried and ground.

## Caramel

Aromatic, piquant flavouring produced by the last but one stage in the boiling of sugar (see **Syrup**); usually used for flavouring sweets.

## Caraway

The pungent, aromatic seed of the *carum carvi,* a biennial plant cultivated in southern Europe for its seed but which grows wild in England. The plant has flat white flower heads, looks like cumin, and the seeds are used in dried form in cakes, bread and biscuits. Some cheeses are also flavoured with caraway.

## Carbonade

A well-known Flemish way of stewing meat, particularly beef, with beer, the top of the dish being covered with crusts of bread that soak up the fat and are crisped golden-brown in the cooking. In the old days it was a dish that was grilled or boiled over the coals (carbone).

## Cardamom

*(Amomum cardamomum)*
A pungent, aromatic spice that comes from small, black seeds usually grouped in fours in the capsules of the cardamom tree. Used mainly in curry flavouring; used pharmaceutically in treating flatulence.

## Cardinal

Designation of sauces or dishes that naturally have a bright red colour, like Lobster Cardinal, or Apples Cardinal (apples with strawberry sauce).

## Cardoon

*(Cynara cardunculus)*
A vegetable of the artichoke family whose crisp white stalks are cooked like sea kale; in fact sea kale is the nearest thing in looks and taste to the cardoon, which is not well-known in England.

## Carmine

(or **Cochineal**)
A bluish-red colouring obtained from the cochineal insect is called cochineal; a brilliant carmine colouring will result if the process is carried further.

## Carp

A family of fresh-water fish; the golden carp is particularly popular in countries remote from the sea and its large-flaked flesh is excellent boiled or braised on a bed of vegetables. The carp family includes such fish as goldfish, chub, tench and bream. The golden carp, 2–4 lb in weight, is much sought after for gefillte fish: the flesh is taken out of the skin, leaving the skin and head intact, and made into a mousse with onions, herbs and water, stuffed back into the skin and the whole braised or poached before being sliced and served with the cooking juices as a sauce.

## Carrageen

One of the edible seaweeds, also called Iberian Moss or Irish Sea Moss. Grows on rocks, light brown in colour, and is spread out in the open to bleach after the salt has been washed out. Rainwater washes it further and it is hung up to dry when creamy white; has a gelatinous texture and can be used instead of isinglass, and can be stewed gently in milk for blancmange or jelly. Regarded highly as an invalid or baby food and was once very popular as a general food.

## Carrot

*(Dancus carota)*
One of the most widely used of all root vegetables with a flavour which, although un-asserting and somewhat mild, is delicate and delicious enough to make the carrot indispensable in an enormous range of recipes from stock to elaborate preserves. It has stood the test of time at least since the days of ancient Greece and its beautiful green leaves are said to have been used as ladies' head dress decorations in the 16th century.

## Cashew

A kidney-shaped nut whose kernel is usually fried in butter, salted, and eaten as a cocktail nut. May be pounded or ground, its piquant flavour adding much to a velouté sauce for poultry.

## Casserole

A cooking vessel with a lid and made of metal, earthenware or other ovenproof material. Designed for slow oven cooking of meat or game. Also the food cooked in a casserole.

## Cassis

A syrup or liqueur made in France from blackcurrant skins.

## Cassolette

Individual container made by deep-frying thin batter on a special mould; filled with savoury mixtures such as shellfish, kidneys, scrambled eggs or cheese.

## Cassoulet

A traditional dish of the Languedoc area of France. Recipes vary with districts, but should contain haricot beans, pickled goose (or some duck) and garlic (or pork) sausage.

## Castle pudding

The same mixture as for Victoria sponge, but baked in a special castle pudding (or dariole) mould and served hot with jam sauce.

## Caudle

A spiced oatmeal gruel with wine added.

## Caul

Foetal membrane. Pigs' and sheep's caul are used for cooking, cleaned and prepared by the butcher. Looks like a thick veil with fat ribbing and is used to protect food and provide fat while cooking.

## Cauliflower

(*Oleracea botrylis*)
A vegetable whose close white flower is encased in leaves of a soft, bright green colour. Some of the outside leaves are best left with the flower when it is cooked to improve flavour and preserve shape. Can be served in many different ways, but usually is boiled gently first, with the flower uppermost. Classic dish is cauliflower cheese, in which boiled cauliflower is covered with a béchamel or white sauce and cheese and browned in the oven (*gratiné mornay*); may be served with golden-fried breadcrumbs sprinkled on it, or with mayonnaise or vinaigrette dressing as a salad, or the flowerets dipped in batter, fried and served with tomato sauce.

## Caviar

Expensive, luxurious roe of the sturgeon; the best comes from Russia. The flavour of the small grey-black eggs is best brought out when served as an hors d'oeuvre with the traditional Russian blinis, or hot toast, quarters of lemon and fresh butter. The caviar should be ice cold; may also be served as a cocktail canapé.

## Cayenne

Chillis dried and ground into hot, red pepper. See **Capsicum**.

## Celeriac

(*Apium rapaceum*)
A very useful vegetable which looks like a turnip but is in fact

root celery; in season late November to end of February. Can be cooked like a turnip, or blanched and eaten as salad.

## Celery
(*Apium graveolens*)
A very popular vegetable, the stalk of which is eaten and the seeds, leaves and root used for flavouring (stews, chutneys, relishes, etc.). Is equally good raw or cooked; British grown celery is in season from late October to January, but it is now imported from late June onwards.

## Cep or Cèpe
(*Boletus edulis*)
A fungus like a large mushroom with shiny brown top, thick cap and spongy gill, and thick white stem. In general it may be treated in the same way as a mushroom, fried in butter, stewed, etc., but because of its size is often stewed as ragoût or the cap removed and cut into slices and fried in olive oil. Is very popular in France, and also grows in Britain but is not often recognised.

## Chafing dish
A frying pan used for cooking

at the table, usually over a spirit lamp, but possibly also over butane gas or electricity. Is deep and generally used for quick dishes (ragoût of kidneys, scrambled eggs, etc.). A favourite for flambé desserts such as crêpes Suzette.

## Chambertin
A Burgundy wine, full-flavoured and rich, which gives its name to certain recipes including Burgundy, for instance chicken cooked in Burgundy with mushrooms is *poulet Chambertin*.

## Chamomile
see Camomile

## Champagne
The sparkling white wine made in the district of the same name in France round Epernay and Rheims. Sugar added to the wine at a certain stage produces a second fermentation and the characteristic sparkle. The process is expensive since a good champagne takes several years to make.

## Chanterelle
(*Cantharellus cibarius*)
An edible fungus, coloured and shaped like a golden trumpet, and plentiful in the woods in early autumn. It has a slightly peppery but good flavour and should be stewed slowly in good stock to overcome toughness. Like ceps, are much sought-after in France, but are betterknown in England than ceps. Again, care should be taken in identification.

## Chantilly
(*crème Chantilly*)
Cream flavoured with vanilla, slightly sweetened, and whipped.

29

## Chapon

A means of flavouring a salad: rub a crust of bread with garlic, place this chapon in the salad, particularly with chicory, and remove just before serving.

## Chapatti

An unleavened Indian bread, flat, baked on a griddle from a well-kneaded paste of flour and water. Generally served with curry.

## Char

Species of small trout, about l lb in weight, with olive-green back, and white and red spots on lighter coloured sides. Was once commonplace in England, and potted char (like potted or soused herring) was a common dish, but nowadays it is rarely seen here. Best known in Switzerland, particularly Lake Geneva.

## Charcoal

A fuel used extensively in the Mediterranean countries for cooking and heating, but mainly for outdoor barbecues in England. Made by burning wood; also used pharmaceutically as an internal disinfectant, once popular for indigestion and flatulence. Gives off poisonous fumes when burning and therefore should be used indoors only with great care.

## Charcuterie

A pork butchery and the class of goods it sells, such as cold meats, mainly pork, e g., brawn, tongues, sausages, galantines, game in aspic.

## Chard (or Sea-kale beet)

The fleshy, long stalks of the chard plant may be tied in bundles and treated like sea-kale or asparagus, while the leaves should be treated like spinach, which they resemble.

## Charlotte

A dessert which may be served hot or cold, but which basically is set in a plain mould, like a cake-tin, deep with sloping sides wider at the top. Examples. *Cold - Charlotte Russe:* Line bottom of mould with jelly made with lemon, raspberry, etc., and place savoy biscuits or sponge fingers round sides as lining; fill with bavarois mixture, turning out when set. In Edwardian times a piece of ribbon was tied round it.

*Hot - Apple Charlotte:* Lay fingers of bread and butter overlapping on bottom and sides of mould, then fill with a marmelade (well-reduced purée) of stone fruit or apple. Bake until bread is crisp, golden-brown and serve hot with custard or fruit sauce.

## Chartreuse

The name of a well-known liqueur which is also applied to a dish that must be moulded and have one main ingredient supplemented by smaller quantities of choicer ingredients. Thus a chartreuse of veal would be a veal mousse with a ham, tongue and mushroom salpicon in the centre. As a sweet it might consist of a lemon jelly with various fruits set in it; in either case it may be set in a ring mould or charlotte mould.

## Chasseur

French word for a huntsman. A dish or sauce cooked with white wine, tomatoes and mushrooms.

## Chateaubriand

This classic dish is a very thick slice cut out of the middle (the coeur or heart) of a fillet of beef, enough for two persons. It is grilled very carefully and served, sliced downwards, with maître d'hôtel butter and château potatoes.

## Chaudfroid

French, meaning 'hot-cold'; a sauce which sets when cold. White chaudfroid is made on the base of a béchamel, milk, some flour and a certain amount of aspic jelly so that it will set. Brown chaudfroid, not often seen nowadays, is based on a demi-glacé sauce. It is always used cold. For instance, chicken chaudfroid is prepared by boiling the chicken then coating with the sauce just before the latter reaches setting point. After decorating with sliced mushroom or truffle, the whole is covered with cool liquid aspic to glaze it.

## Chausson

A turnover. A piece of short or flaky pastry is rolled out into a flat, round piece and half of it covered with jam or fruit. The other half is folded over it and the edges crimped to seal, then the chausson is baked and allowed to cool before eating. It may also consist of two pieces of pastry with a sandwich filling.

## Cheddar

One of the best-known English cheeses, keeps well and travels well. A large, hard cheese with many imitators.

## Cheese

There are two types of cheese, hard and soft, both from milk solids in curd form. Hard cheeses include the familiar English Cheddar, Cheshire and Stilton, and Continental cheese like Parmesan. Most of the soft cheeses are Continental, like Camembert and Brie from France. Gorgonzola and Roquefort, although of creamy consistency, are classed as hard. See also **Brie, Camembert, Cheddar, Cheshire, Gorgonzola, Gruyère, Parmesan, Roquefort, Stilton** and **Wensleydale**.

## Cherry

A small stone fruit ripening in England in summer, but also imported outside the English season. There are three main types of English cherry, mostly grown in the Home Counties and Kent: May Dukes, white hearts and Morellos. They ripen in that order, from late June to the end of July. For dessert the May Dukes, red with firm flesh, and the white hearts (*Bigarreau*)

31

## Chestnut
(or **Spanish chestnut**)
Most of the chestnuts used in cookery in Britain are imported from Italy and France, being large and floury when cooked; those grown in England usually are too small for practical use. If taken whole after being shelled and cooked, the chestnut may be made into the famous *marron glacé* with sugar syrup, or braised, or if mashed or sieved may be used for sweet or savoury purposes, in cakes, stuffings and purées.

## Chick pea
A large yellow dried pea popular in Mediterranean countries for stews and soups. They need long soaking, then long, slow cooking, like the haricot bean. Also like the haricot they are said to be very nutritious.

## Chicken
Domestic bird reared both for eating and for laying eggs; its description depends on the age at which it is killed. Nowadays for eating purposes chickens are usually sold in the shops already dressed, and their weight is in that state, plus the weight of giblets; it is usually marked on oven-ready birds.
*Poussin* Not more than about $1\frac{1}{4}$ lb, aged 4–6 weeks, killed for boning, stuffing and roasting, grilling, frying, pot-roasting etc., will feed only one person. Two people may be served from a double poussin, not more than 2 lb and about 8–10 weeks old.
*Spring chicken* (*Broiler*) About $2–2\frac{1}{2}$ lb, 3 months old; cooked like poussins, or sautéd.
*Roasting chicken* Up to about 4 lb, about 1 year old and usable

are used. The former may also be made into compotes, but the white hearts lose their flavour when cooked. The Morellos, despite their highly attractive appearance, are best used for preserving. To conserve their considerable juice they are cut from the tree, leaving only a short stalk which, if pulled later, should bring out the stone with it, thus saving the tart, slightly acid flesh.

## Cherry brandy
Well-known liqueur made from Morello cherries infused in brandy.

## Chervil
(*Anthriscus cerefolium*)
Hardy annual herb whose flavour resembles aniseed. Its leaves are small and bright green, in sprays somewhat like maidenhair fern, and are sometimes used for decoration of cold dishes. The flavour of chervil is used in *sauce béarnaise.*

## Cheshire
One of the hard English cheeses, red or white, made from cow's milk.

for almost any dish involving chicken. Most widely found.

*Boiling fowl* An older bird, probably already used for laying, say 18 months old, which lends itself better to boiling or stewing. Tends to be very fatty.

*Cockerel* Male bird, should be killed when about 6 months old, unless treated as a capon. See appendix diagrams

## Chicken turbot
see **Turbot**

## Chicory
(*Cichorium endiva*)
A winter vegetable in season from November to March; may be eaten raw or cooked. Imported into England, mainly from Belgium. Some confusion arises over the name: what is called chicory in England is known as *endive* in France, whereas the curly endive used in salads in England is called *chicorée frisée* in France. Chicory used to mix with coffee is entirely different; it is the roasted and ground root of the *Intybus* plant.

## Chiffonade
Green vegetables such as lettuce, sorrel, spinach, etc., cut up into shreds (*chiffon* in French means rag) to form a bed for dishes such as egg mayonnaise.

## Chilli
Chilli powder is ground from the dried small red chilli. See also **Capsicum**.

## Chine
The backbone of an animal (from the French *échine*, meaning spinal column). Butchers usually saw through the bone when preparing cutlets or a roast on the ribs or loin.

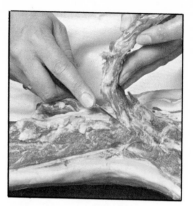

## Chinese gooseberry
A fruit with flesh, seeds and flavour resembling a gooseberry. Is usually on sale in England for Christmas; is oval, shaped like a sausage and has a brown skin.

## Chip
A piece of fried potato, generally named according to its size and shape. Thus game chips are potatoes sliced wafer-thin and fried; *allumettes* are shaped like matchsticks; straw potatoes (*pommes pailles*) are cut in long thin strips or straws; *pont neuf* are thick fingers of potato.

## Chipolata
Nowadays generally accepted as a smaller and thinner version of the ordinary sausage, but in Italy was a rich, onion-flavoured ragoût and in French was from the word *ciboule*, meaning chive.

## Chitterling
Small pieces of offal, or intestine, of a freshly slaughtered animal, fried.

## Chive
(*Allium schoenoprasum*)
Fleshy green shoots from small bulbs which are grown in

33

clusters for their delicate onion flavour, which makes them a delicious addition to salads and stuffings. Only the shoots are cut, with scissors, from the clusters which may be in pots or in the garden.

## Chocolate

Chocolate is milled from cocoa in a highly skilled process, the quality, and therefore the price, being dependent on the amount of milling, added sugar, and starch involved. Usually sold in blocks, but may be in powder form. Eating chocolate is sold in many forms, but for cooking it is plain or unsweetened; the former has some sugar in it, the latter does not and is usually sold only through wholesalers.

## Chop

The name given to a piece of meat cut from the loin of lamb, mutton, veal or pork, up to about $1\frac{1}{2}$ in thick; if taken from the part of the loin nearest the tail it is called a chump chop (there are only two in each side of the animal). In chump chops there is more bone than in others.

## Choucroûte

French, meaning sauerkraut (fermented cabbage). A dish of this, with boiled pork or ham, and other garnishes such as garlic sausage, is known as *choucroûte garnie*.

## Choux

One of the most important basic pastry mixtures, made with fat, flour, water and eggs. May be baked in spoonfuls, or *petits choux*, for profiteroles, or in lengths from a forcing bag for *éclairs*, or deep fried in small sweet or savoury *beignets*.

## Chowder

A soup made from shellfish, a seaboard speciality in the eastern United States. In addition to clams, lobster, etc., or white fish, it may also have salt pork, onions and other vegetables. There are many variations, as with bouillabaisse in France, but the fish should be fresh.

## Chutney

A condiment, usually containing a mixture of many sweet and sour ingredients like fruits, sugar, spices and vinegar which have been cooked slowly for a long time. Indian in origin and may be hot, or mild. Some are bottled for keeping but others are made fresh for immediate use.

## Cider

Fermented apple juice. Made extensively in places where apples are widely cultivated, such as England, France (Normandy), Canada and the U.S.A. May be drunk alone or in a cup or punch. Draught cider is much stronger and heady than the bottled type. For cooking purposes draught cider is better and is used in soups, stews, and in making vinegar. Also used to improve the flavour of apple fritter batter.

# Cinnamon

A warm, sweet aromatic spice suitable for adding to sweet foods and drinks. Sold either in quills or sticks, or ground into powder, the former used in mulled wine, spiced fruits, etc., the latter in cakes or pastry, or for flavouring some fruits. Most comes from the bark of the *Cinnamomum zeylanicum,* a tree growing in Ceylon and the Malabar coast, but a slightly more bitter type comes from the *Cinnamomum cassia,* or cassia tree.

# Citron

A citrus fruit, large, lemon-shaped and with a thick rind which has a dark green, translucent appearance when candied, for which the citron is extensively used. Is used in mixed peel and, candied and sliced thin, for decorating a Madeira cake.

# Civet

French, meaning a rich game stew; the French equivalent of jugged hare is *civet de lièvre.* See also **Hare**.

# Clafouti

A dessert which originated in the Provence region of France; cherries, red or black, are covered with a thick batter after being stoned and laid in a dish, and are then baked.

# Clam

Well-known shellfish, generally regarded as American although it is sometimes found on English coasts. Looks something like a large mussel and is cooked similarly to the mussel; the main ingredient of chowder, but may also be baked.

# Claret

The English name for red wine from the Bordeaux region of France.

# Clarify

To remove impurities. By adding water (about $\frac{1}{3}$ the quantity) to fat or dripping, boiling the whole and allowing it to cool, it will be found that impurities have passed into the water and the fat, in a solid piece, will have been clarified, or cleansed. See **Butter**. Egg whites added to meat broths like consommé, or to jellies, have the same effect. Egg whites are whisked in as the mixture is brought to the boil; they coagulate and rise to the top, carrying any opaque matter with them. Poured through a jelly bag the liquid should become clear, or clarified.

# Clementine

see **Orange**

# Clod

see **Beef** diagram in appendix

# Clove

*(Eugenia carophyllata)*
1. An aromatic spice, the name coming from the Latin *clovus* meaning a nail, which the clove resembles before it is ground. In fact it is the bud of a shrub which grows in the Spice Islands (Moluccas). An onion

stuck with cloves is a classic flavouring for soups, stews and sauces.

2. A segment of **Garlic.**

# Coal fish, Coly or Saithe

A fish common in English fish shops, caught in the north. Is not unlike a haddock, with black skin, grey flesh, the latter turning white when cooked. For eating should be small and young.

# Cob nut

see **Filbert**

# Cochineal

see **Carmine**

# Cockerel

see **Chicken**

# Cockle

Small shellfish with ribbed white shells, which are hinged. Boiled and usually eaten cold with bread, butter and vinegar. Generally sold ready cooked in fishmongers where mussels, whelks and other molluscs are found.

# Cocoa

The cocoa tree grows in tropical countries and has a pod which contains seeds, or nibs, which are roasted and milled to produce cocoa or chocolate. The quality of cocoa or chocolate depends on how much of a

sweet-scented, yellowish fat is extracted during milling or is added with starch and sugar after milling. This fat is called **Cocoa Butter.** A special drink for children may be made by infusing the nib, but for general purposes powdered cocoa is made into a hot drink, being more digestible than the richer chocolate.

# Coconut

The fruit of the *Cocas nucifera* or coconut palm which grows in the eastern parts of Asia and the East Indies; large, with hairy husk and tough shell. Inside is a crisp white flesh and some slightly greenish liquid which makes a refreshing drink. (This is not coconut milk referred to in some curry recipes, which is simply milk infused with coconut for more flavouring.) Dried or desiccated and grated, the coconut flesh is used for confectionery, cakes, curries, chutnies and so on.

# Cod

One of the commonest deep sea fish. Can weigh anything from about 1½ lb up to 20 lb, the best being about 9–10 lb and fished between May and October, although cod are available all year round. The flesh, usually bought in steaks or fillets, is in large flakes, the roe sold fresh or smoked and the liver used for cod liver oil. The tongues used to be regarded as a delicacy. Some fillets are

salted and dried for export to countries, particularly in the Mediterranean, which prefer them that way; or cod may be smoked and used as a cheaper substitute for smoked haddock. Salt cod must be well soaked before cooking. The fresh fish is greatly improved if rubbed with lemon, salted and left for an hour, then drained before being cooked in any of the wide range of recipes to which it lends itself. See also **Brandade**.

# Coffee

The beans of the coffee berry, when dried, roasted and ground, provide the coffee with which we are familiar and which is prepared in almost as many ways as there are cooks. The extent of roasting determines the taste: the Continental roast favoured by the French is burned almost black while others are only lightly roasted; there are also blends. The beans are ground according to whether the coffee will be made in a percolator, filter, by the vacuum method, or etc.

# Cognac

The name given to a fine brandy produced under strictly controlled rules from the grapes of a relatively small area of France, of which the small town of Cognac is the centre, in the Charente district. See also **Brandy, Eau-de-vie**.

# Cointreau

An orange-flavoured liqueur made in France.

# Colcannon

An Irish dish of mashed potato beaten with cooked and chopped cabbage, butter and milk until the mixture is fluffy and very light.

# Cole slaw

A crisp cabbage, shredded, chilled, and mixed with mayonnaise or cream, with a garnish for serving of green peppers, apple, etc. Originated in the United States.

# Coly

see **Coal Fish**

# Compote

Fruit such as apple, gooseberry, apricot, etc., which has been poached in syrup usually made of sugar and water.

# Concasser

To chop up, especially tomatoes. First remove skin and seeds, then chop flesh roughly.

# Condensed milk

Canned milk, usually sweetened. The process used renders the milk thick, to a consistency similar to honey.

# Condiment

Spices and seasonings to add flavour and piquancy to a dish, such as salt, pepper, mustard or bottled sauces.

37

# Conger eel

see **Eel**

# Consommé

A concentrated, clarified soup made from beef and bone stock. The names of various consommés depend on their garnishes, eg. *petite marmite*, with chicken. A cold consommé sets to a jelly.

# Continental sausages

The number of different types of Continental sausages on sale here increases as delicatessens cater for wider ranges of taste. The better-known ones, mostly made of pork, are:

*Liver* Usually richer and with more flavour than the English varieties, the most popular are from Germany, Belgium and France.

*Salami* Made in many continental countries, particularly Hungary, Germany and Italy, varies in flavour, consistency and garlic content. Usually speckled in appearance because of particles of fat among the red meat.

*Garlic* French sausage, made of salted pork or ham with heavy garlic flavouring, about 3 in diameter.

*Mortadella* Originally Italian, very large and rather soft in texture. These are all used in or as hors d'oeuvre and mostly are served cold and very thinly sliced. **Saveloys** and **Frankfurters** are not served this way.

# Coriander

The dried and powdered fruit of the coriander tree *Coriandrum sativum* is one of the spices used in curries. Sometimes the ripe seeds and the leaves of the tree are used fresh, but sparingly because of their pungent, oily flavour. Candied seeds may be eaten as comfits.

# Corned beef

'Corns' are crystals of coarse salt used in pickling; thus a 'corned' meat is one which has been pickled in such salt. Corned beef is generally boiled.

# Cornet

see **Mould**

# Cornish pasty

A turnover of short or flaky pastry, enough for one or up to 4 persons, with a filling of meat, onions and potatoes.

# Cornflour

A fine starch obtained by milling the kernel of Indian corn or maize. May be used for blancmanges, and for thickening sauces, gravies, etc. Mixed with wheat flour in making some types of cake.

# Corn-on-the-cob

see **Indian Corn**

# Corn salad

(or **Lamb's lettuce**)

A small annual vegetable named *Valerianella olitoria,* which, although not very tasty in itself, makes a very useful addition to other winter vegetables in a salad. The plant is not affected by frost and is pulled whole and washed before being included in the salad.

# Coulibiaca

A typical Russian dish: a long, fat roll of brioche dough or puff pastry enclosing a mixture of flaked salmon and rice well glazed with beaten egg and baked. Should be covered with a sauce suprême or cream sauce and served hot.

## Coulis

A concentrated soup or stew of meat or vegetables.

## Coupe

A silver or glass cup, usually on a stem, for serving ice cream, fruit salads, etc. Followed by a name, eg. Coupe française, it denotes the type of dessert.

## Courgette

**(or Zucchini)**
A miniature type of marrow, cooked the same way but usually without peeling. They have a delicate flavour, are easily grown, maturing at the same time as marrows. Imported courgettes are available for most of the year.

## Court bouillon

A stock made of water, wine or vinegar and root vegetables. This slightly acidulated liquid is used for poaching fish, veal, etc., since it keeps flesh a good colour and adds flavour.

## Cous-cous

There are numerous recipes for this Arabian dish, which consists essentially of a type of millet flour cooked in water until fluffy and served with a stew of mutton.

## Crab

The crab commonly sold in England ranges from 1 to 3½ lb in weight, with large claws and a rough, reddish-brown shell. Crabs are usually sold cooked and are moderate in price, but if required for salad with mayon-

naise, etc., they must be dressed. This is a somewhat complex operation and the instructions in the cookery book should be closely followed; or the fishmonger may do it for an extra charge. Crab meat, both white and dark or mixed, may also be bought fresh or frozen by the pound. This is used in soufflés, savouries, etc. The fresh crab season is May to September.

## Crab-apple

A small apple which grows wild or on trees cultivated mainly for decoration. Makes a delicious jelly or spiced fruit, but has a very bitter flavour and is not eaten raw. The tree blossom is white or pale pink; the fruit ranges from scarlet to golden-yellow.

## Crackling

The skin of roast pork. Before cooking the skin is scored with the point of a sharp knife, so that the fat becomes crisp.

## Cranberry

Cranberry sauce, made from the red berry of the shrub which grows wild on moorland or may be cultivated, is the traditional accompaniment to turkey in the U.S.A. Also used in jellies.

# Crapaudine
Spatchcock. Small birds split down the back and flattened for cooking, usually grilling.

# Crawfish
This is the French *langouste*, or rock lobster, a crustacean which may weigh 3–6 lb and is more popular on the Continent than in England. It has a rough brown-red shell and small claws. Its flesh, coarser than that of lobster, is all in the tail and is cut into 'scallops' for serving. Because of its size, often used for a *pièce montée* or centrepiece on a cold table.

# Crayfish
Small, lobster-like shellfish found in fresh waters, particularly in Scandinavia, where it is so popular that it is given a festival each year. Usually boiled and served with dressing and bread and butter. Called *écrevisse* in France.

# Cream
If milk is allowed to stand, the fat, or cream, rises to the top. Commercially the fats are separated mechanically from the milk, in various proportions to give different types of cream. Pasteurisation by heat treatment will make it difficult to separate cream from milk. The various types of cream that may be encountered are:
*Fresh cream* This is the source of all other creams; will keep for 48 hours, but is better used on the day it is bought.
*Single cream* Must have at least 18 per cent butterfat content; may be homogenised for even suspension of fat globules.
*Whipping cream* Must have 38 per cent butterfat content, making it possible to be whipped.
*Double cream* Minimum 48 per cent butterfat.
*Soured cream* Used in making butter, cream cheese, etc., and in some recipes, especially mid-European dishes such as **Bortsch, Goulash.**
*Clotted cream* Made by leaving milk to stand for about 12 hours until cream rises, then heating slowly to scalding point; the milk is then taken off the heat and allowed to stand until the cream clots, or thickens, and is skimmed off. Clotted cream is a speciality of Devon and Cornwall; Devonshire cream is smoother and more solid than the Cornish.
*Ultra-heat-treated* A special high temperature treatment makes it possible to keep fresh cream for three months.
*Canned cream* Fresh pasteurised cream, homogenised and sealed in cans keeps indefinitely.
*Frozen cream* Cream frozen at very high speed will keep at or below 32°F (0°C), but once thawed must be treated like fresh cream and not refrozen.
*Synthetic cream* Made from fats and edible oils other than milk and used mainly for decoration or soufflés.

# Cream of tartar
A chemical, potassium bitartrate, which when mixed with bicarbonate of soda and moistened releases carbonic acid gas; therefore, used as a raising agent. To prevent graining when boiling syrup, a pinch of cream of tartar may be used instead of liquid glucose.

# Crécy
Because carrots grown in the

region of this French town are renowned, some dishes containing carrots are said to be cooked *à la Crécy*.

## Crème Chantilly
see **Chantilly**

## Crème de menthe
A peppermint flavoured liqueur.

## Crème pâtissière
see **Pastry Cream**

## Crémet
A speciality of the Dauphinois district of France: a milk curd made without becoming too sour is beaten with egg whites and cream, sweetened and drained in special pots.

## Creole
Meat or chicken garnished with rice cooked with tomatoes and peppers like a pilaf.

## Crêpe
see **Pancake**

## Crêpe Suzette
A pancake made from batter flavoured with curaçao, cooked very thin and spread with a mixture of butter and sugar, and the juice and zest of either an orange or a tangerine. After being folded the pancakes are flamed with either more curaçao or brandy.

## Cress
(**Garden Cress** or *Lepidium satirum*)
A quick growing, small plant which springs up easily from small seed, even on a damp flannel inside the house. Useful for sandwiches (egg and cress), salads or garnishes. See also **Watercress** and **Mustard**.

## Croissant
Traditional French breakfast roll, rich, flaky and with a distinctive crescent (*croissant*) shape. Made from a dough of flour, water, milk and yeast which is first allowed to rise and then rolled with butter as for puff pastry, and baked with butter.

## Croque-en-Bouche
French meaning 'crack-in-the-mouth'. An elaborate dessert made by coating small crisp balls of baked choux pastry or meringue with sugar syrup boiled to the crack stage. They are then stacked up into a pyramid about 8 in high, topped with spun sugar and the space in the middle either filled with crème Chantilly or left empty.

## Croquette
Cooked and chopped chicken, hard-boiled eggs or flaked fish in a savoury mixture bound together with a thick béchamel sauce. The mixture is divided and rolled into balls or flat rounds, dipped in egg and breadcrumbs and deep fried. See also **Rissole**.

## Croustade
Bread hollowed out and fried in deep fat to form a casing for savoury mixtures. May be made from a whole loaf with the crust cut off, or thick slices. The filling might consist of, say, prawns and buttered eggs, or sweetbreads, etc. The croustade may or may not be eaten, according to taste.

## Croûte
A piece of bread toasted or fried to be used as a base for a savoury mixture, or a garnish for a dish with a rich gravy, for

instance *boeuf à la bourguig-nonne*. Generally the bread is in thin slices and cut in triangles. See also **Canapé**.

## Croûton
A small piece or cube of fried bread or potato, generally served with cream or purée soups.

## Crowdie
A Scottish cheese made from soured milk curd.

## Crudités
The French name for a dish of raw spring onions, carrots, radishes and other vegetables served at the beginning of a lunch.

## Crumpet
A form of pancake made from a yeast batter baked on special rings in a quick oven. Crumpets are thick and about 3 in in diameter, the method of baking producing one side smooth and the other full of small holes.

They are generally served at tea time, toasted and with plenty of butter; sometimes, particularly in winter, they may be served with bacon. (Known in some areas as pikelets.)

## Crustacea
A general term for all shellfish.

## Crystallisation
As some confectionery, such as glacé fruits and fondant creams, are finished they are given an attractive as well as protective coating by crystalli-sation of sugar. This requires a saccharometer to make sure that the syrup is between 32° and 36° and a thermometer to ensure that it has boiled to 220–224°F. When it has cooled the syrup is poured over the fruits or fondants to be coated, in special trays; they remain for some time in the syrup and when drained and dried should be completely coated with crystals.

# Cucumber

A type of melon grown as a salad vegetable, mostly under glass in England; available all year round but most plentiful from May to September. Some outdoor cucumbers are used for pickling.

# Cuisson

Juices from cooking meat, poultry or fish.

# Cullis

See **Coulis**

# Cummin

(*Cumminum cyminum*)
Seeds used for flavouring and in making some liqueurs. Very like caraway in appearance and taste.

# Curaçao

An orange-flavoured liqueur made from gin or brandy and the rind of Seville oranges.

# Curds

Curds are milk solids which appear when milk turns sour or when acid is added and the milk heated. Soft curds are produced by adding rennet, as for junket; addition of a cheese rennet produces the hard curds which are the basis for cheese-making, but cream cheese can be made from the softish curds of soured milk. See also **Crowdie**.

# Curing

Meat and fish may be subjected to the process of curing with salt, sugar and saltpetre in order to preserve them. They may be dry salted or pickled in a brine, the important ingredient being salt; the saltpetre is used only to give the meat colour, and sugar to counteract the hardening effect of saltpetre. Hams, bacon, kippers, bloaters and haddock are first cured in salt and then further preserved by smoking.

# Currant

An acid-flavoured soft fruit which ripens in July. *Black currants* have a high vitamin C content and are extensively used for making a cordial or syrup, also for jams, jellies, and tarts; Cassis is made from this fruit. *Red currants* make the traditional jelly served with meat or game, and also syrup drinks. *White currants* are less common but also used in sweets, jellies and syrups. All have a high pectin content. Dried currants are the fruit of the Corinth grape.

# Curry

A strongly spiced eastern dish or sauce. In Britain the spices are sold ready ground and mixed as curry powder. In India the cook would mix his own spices according to the food to be cooked. The main spices used are cayenne, coriander, turmeric, cumin, ginger, mace, cloves, cardamom, fenugreek and pepper.

# Custard

An egg and milk mixture served as a pudding or a sauce, or forming the basis of a cold soufflé or cream dessert. A custard pudding (caramel custard, for instance) must have whole eggs mixed with egg yolks so as to set into a pudding when it is cooked. For a sauce, only the yolks are used.

# Cutlet

In the case of lamb (or mutton) this is taken from the best end of neck; in veal it might also come from the leg, or a thick fillet. Because they have a delicious flavour and are easily cooked, cutlets are excellent for grills and sautés. Cutlets should be well trimmed of fat before grilling or sautéing.

## Cutlet bat

A heavy, flat, metal bat with a handle, for flattening fillets of fish, escalopes, cutlets, etc., before they are cooked.

## Cuttlefish

see **Octopus**

## Dab

A fish of the flounder species, flat and small, about 4–6 oz in weight, caught on sandy shores round Britain.

## Damson

A type of plum, small and purple, with a delicious rich flavour when cooked and excellent for preserves of all kinds, particularly jams, jellies, compotes and fruit cheeses, but not very good uncooked. Ripening from August to mid-September.

## Dandelion

A weed whose leaves, when taken young and blanched like chicory, are excellent in a salad, either by themselves or with other greens. May be cultivated to get strong plants, or wild plants can be used.

## Dariole

see **Mould**

## Darne

A thick slice of fish weighing at least 2 lb, taken from the middle of a cod, turbot or salmon.

## D'Artois

Two pieces of puff pastry filled with fruit and pastry cream, baked and sliced.

## Date

Soft, sweet and pulpy dried fruit, said to be very nutritious, from the date palm tree. Lesser quality fruit are compressed after being stoned, and sold by weight for puddings and cakes, but the best quality are packed traditionally in oblong boxes and sold as dessert fruit, particularly for Christmas. Cultivated chiefly in North Africa.

## Daube

A dish, usually of beef, which has been well seasoned and braised in red wine for several hours.

## Dauphinois

A dish with a large proportion of cheese and milk or cream. *Gratin dauphinois* consists of milk, Gruyère cheese and thin slices of potato cooked in the oven.

## Deglaze

To heat stock and/or wine in a roasting pan, together with the remaining sediment or deposits from roasting or sautéing to make a sauce or gravy.

## Dégorger
A process which, like blanching, is aimed at removing any strong taste from a food. Vegetables like cucumbers or aubergines are sliced, lightly salted, allowed to stand for an hour or so, then well drained before cooking.

## Demi-deuil
Literally 'half-mourning'. Very thin slices of truffle are forced under the skin on the breast of a chicken or turkey and left for some hours before the bird is roasted. The smell of the truffles penetrates the skin.

## Demi-glace
Rich brown sauce made from bone stock reduced to the consistency of syrup. When meat or game entrées are coated with it, it forms a half-glaze (*demi glace*). See also **Brown Sauce.** May also be served as a sauce with grilled or roasted meat.

## Dépouiller
In making a demi-glace sauce, scum or grease is forced to the surface by pouring in small quantities of cold stock as the sauce simmers. This scum is skimmed off and thus the sauce is *dépouillé* (literally 'skinned') until it finally becomes rich brown and semi-clear.

## Dessert
In modern meals usually the sweet course, but in formal banquets it is the last course. This is served after the tablecloth, condiments, etc., have been removed. Guests are given dessert plates and cutlery and served with fresh and dried fruits, nuts and a dessert wine, such as port. Finger bowls are also placed on the table.

## Devil
Devilled food is food that has been made peppery, spiced, hot in taste. This is done either by marinating, eg. in Worcestershire sauce or a mixture of sauces, or by 'dry devilling'— peppering and spreading with mustard—before cooking. The process can be applied to poultry, game, fish or meat. Joints should be fried in butter, or buttered and grilled and be almost charred before being served. Devil or barbecue sauce may be served separately.

## Dhal
Lentils, well-seasoned, flavoured with some curry powder or green ginger and made into a purée. Served with curry.

## Dice
To cut meat, fruit or vegetables into small squares.

## Dill
A delicately flavoured annual herb with feathery, grey-green leaves. Goes well with fish, either in a sauce or sprinkled over; is more delicate and subtle than fennel and marries well with cucumber. The stalks and seeds are used in pickles, particularly cucumber, and the seeds for flavouring salads and vegetables.

## Dolmas (or Dolmades)

Vine leaves (and by extension cabbage leaves) stuffed with minced lamb and cooked in stock. May be finished with strong tomato sauce. Both in the original Turkish and also in Greek the word is now applied to most kinds of food cooked in a roly-poly shape.

## Dough

Basic mixture of flour, liquid and fat for making bread, scones pastry, etc. Dough should be very light; the liquid used is generally water or milk. See also **Kneading**.

## Doughnut

A nut of bun or bread dough shaped into a ball or ring, fried in deep fat and rolled in caster sugar. It is traditional to press a spoonful of firm jam into the doughnut before it is cooked. Sometimes decorated with fresh, whipped cream.

## Dragée

A small sweetmeat coated with sugar. Almond dragées, for instance, are almonds coated with hard sugar, in white or a pastel colour.

## Drambuie

A liqueur made in Scotland from a whisky and honey base.

## Dredge

To cover liberally with sifted flour or sugar. Usually done from a container which has holes in the top of a size corresponding to the purpose for which it is used, ie, large for flour, very small for icing sugar, etc.

## Dripping

The name given to the fat recovered after roasting meat, beef being the best for most purposes. Since the fat must be kept free of other substances it is strained and allowed to set into a hard cake and the gravy scraped from the bottom. Dripping can then be used for roasting and frying, and beef dripping for shortening cakes and pastry. Generally the gravy remnants are used for enriching soups and stews.

## Drop scone
(or **Pancake**)

Called pancakes in Scotland, the drop scone is made by dropping a thick batter of flour, eggs and milk on to a girdle to produce a scone $\frac{1}{4}-\frac{1}{2}$ in thick and $2\frac{1}{2}$ in or more in diameter. The scone is flat and spongy.

## Duchesse

Potato which has been boiled, made into a purée with butter, hot milk and egg yolk, piped into whatever shape is required, brushed with beaten egg and put in the oven to be browned. It may be piped directly on to the serving dish as a border, or in shapes on a baking sheet.

## Duck

There are two main varieties of this water bird:

*Domestic ducks* are reared for the table and their average weight dressed is 4–5 lb, but because they have shallow breasts compared with chicken, this is only enough for 4 people. The Aylesbury duck, large and white, is regarded as the finest. Usually roasted, the classic accompaniments are sage and onion stuffing, apple sauce, peas and new potatoes.

*Wild duck* are game and available during the season, September 1 to February 28. Because of their diet they tend to have a fishy flavour. Usually roasted, but left underdone (*saignant*) and served with orange salad and a sharp sauce.

## Dugléré

Turbot, sole or other white fish poached in white wine and water and served with a sauce made from the poaching liquid. Cream, concassé tomatoes and chopped parsley are added to the sauce.

## Dulse

One of the edible seaweeds, red-brown in colour, stewed like laver.

## Dumpling

Small ball of paste made from flour, water and salt, cooked by simmering in boiling water or stock. Dumplings are popular in Germany, where they may take sweet or savoury forms and be made of shortcrust, bread, etc; in England suet dumplings are the classic accompaniment to boiled beef.

## Duxelles

A mince of mushrooms, chopped shallots and herbs, cooked in butter and used to flavour soups, sauces and stuffings. The name is said to have come from La Varenne, a famous 17th century chef, in honour of his master, the Marquis d'Uxelles.

# E

## Eau-de-vie

Alcoholic drink made by distilling wine. The best-known is from the wines of the Charente, called Cognac (see also **Brandy**). Many liqueurs also have an eau-de-vie base.

## Eccles cake

A pastry made of two rounds of flaky pastry filled with a rich mixture of dried fruit, mainly currants and candied peel, slashed across the top and glazed with egg white and sugar before being baked. The Eccles cake is kept in a round shape. The Banbury cake is made similarly, but whereas the Eccles cake has filling between two layers of pastry, the Banbury has only one layer of pastry, which is wrapped round the filling and the whole made into an oval shape.

## Eclair

A 3–4 in length of choux pastry

47

piped from a forcing bag and baked until crisp and hollow inside. The éclair is then filled with vanilla, coffee or chocolate pastry cream and a similarly flavoured fondant or glacé icing finishes the top. Pastry cream is the traditional filling, but fresh cream may be used.

## Ecrevisse
French name for cravfish.

## Eel
A long thin fish with a rich, delicate flesh, average weight $1\frac{1}{2}$–2 lb, caught in fresh or salt water, the former being better known. Many are imported into England from Holland either fresh or smoked, the latter being a delicacy and an excellent hors d'oeuvre when sliced thinly. The giant or Conger eel, which may be anything up to 20 feet long, once figured prominently in English fish and chip shops and is a must in the French bouillabaisse.

## Egg
The egg is not only one of the most extensively used but also one of the most valuable kitchen ingredients, its low price and high protein content providing an economical and well-balanced meal. The egg is an essential ingredient in many cakes and puddings and can be prepared in dozens of different ways.
*Hen eggs* Average weight is about 2 oz. 'New Laid' should mean not more than one week old, after which they should be used for cooking.
*Duck (and goose) eggs* Available in spring and summer, duck eggs now are used mainly in cakes, partly because of their size (average weight of a duck egg is $2\frac{1}{2}$ oz, a goose egg up to 4 oz) and partly because they have possible unpleasant effects unless really fresh. Goose eggs are useful for omelets or scrambled eggs, one being enough for two helpings.

To tell a fresh egg, break it and inspect the white: if it clings to the yolk it is fresh; the more liquid the yolk the less fresh the egg.

## Eggplant
see **Aubergine**

## Elderberry
A small black berry used to make wine, syrup or jelly; comes from the elder tree (*Sambucus*) and is picked in September.

# Elderflower

The flower of the elder which, when incorporated into a jelly or syrup, imparts a delicious flavour like that of muscat grapes. A few flowers tied in muslin and stewed with gooseberries gives a flavour that goes extremely well with that fruit. A few gooseberries will also give the right amount of sharpness to elderflower syrup, made by infusing the leaves in a syrup, adding the gooseberries, straining, bottling and sterilising. It may be kept in bottled form and used sparingly to give added flavour to strawberries, fruit salads, etc. The flowers as well as the berries may be used for wine-making.

# Emmenthal
see **Gruyère**

# Endive
see **Chicory**

# Entrecôte

The French name for the cut of beef, full of flavour and tender, which comes from the top part of the ribs of beef, or sirloin. May be served as steaks or a small roast.

# Entrée

The dish which used to follow the fish course and precede the roast, but in modern menus is more likely to appear as the main course. It is a dish which calls for some culinary expertise and is complete in itself, like a meat dish with a vegetable garnish.

# Entremets

Something served as a separate course after the main dish (French, meaning 'between dishes') and before the dessert, possibly a dressed vegetable like asparagus or globe artichoke, or a sweet.

# Epigramme

Small pieces of lamb taken from the breast or best end of neck, simmered, and when tender boned and pressed. When cold they are dipped in egg and breadcrumbs and fried or grilled, then served with a piquant sauce.

# Escalope

A thin slice of meat cut from a fillet, or from the leg, usually veal. Can be cooked in numerous ways.

# Escargot
see **Snail**

# Escarole

*(chicorée scarole)*
The Batavian endive, smooth and green-leaved, as distinct from the curly variety, or *chicorée frisée* (see **Chicory**). It is used as a winter salad.

# Espagnole

One of the basic sauces, or *sauces mères*. It is rich and brown and made with a mirepoix and a fonds brun. A glass of sherry and some strong tomato pulp is added after the sauce has been skimmed and strained.

# Estouffade

A clear but strong broth (see **Fonds Brun**). The name is also given to a beef stew.

# Evaporated milk
see **Condensed Milk**

## Fagot (or Faggot)
1. Minced liver and other meat strongly seasoned, baked and sold in squares, usually to be heated up again before eating.
2. A bunch of herbs.

## Farce
Name given to various stuffings. Used as a verb means to stuff.

## Fat
In one form or another fat is one of the most essential ingredients in cookery, since without it food would be dull, not very nutritious and not tasty. For general cookery purposes fat refers to animal fats like lard; mutton or beef fats, while vegetable and other fats are **Oil** (including such things as groundnut, maize, almond and others that have been treated to remove odour, and olive oil). See also **Butter, Margarine, Suet, Cream.**

## Fécule
Arrowroot, potato flour or other fine starch.

## Fennel
1. A herb, *Foeniculum vulgare,* easily grown as a perennial in gardens in England and used in sparse quantities in fish sauces.
2. A white, bulbous annual root grown in the south of France and Italy (*Foeniculum dulce*) where the climate is sunny enough to mature it. Sliced raw in a salad it has an aniseed flavour, but when cooked as a vegetable the flavour is more delicate. Also called Florence fennel or finocchio.

## Fenugreek
*(Trigonella)*
The seeds of this plant are usually among the spices that go to make up a curry powder.

## Fermière
Meat braised or pot-roasted and garnished with root vegetables like onions, carrots, celery, turnip, cooked with or apart from the meat.

## Fettucine
One of the pastas, ribbon-shaped.

## Feuilleton
see **Fleuron**

## Fig
A fruit grown mostly round the Mediterranean, usually imported into England in dried form and soaked prior to cooking. Some English gardens have trees which bear the oval green fig and some fresh figs of the black, round variety are imported late in the year.

## Filbert
*(Corylus maxima)*
A large nut whose kernel is used similarly to the hazelnut. Also called a cob and used for dessert.

## Fillet
A slice of choice meat, poultry,

or fish without bone. In beef, fillet comes from the undercut of the sirloin. In poultry, it is the small piece of white meat next to the bone (*filet mignon*) or the breast and wing flesh together. In fish, fillets are the flesh on each side of the backbone. Flat fish like sole, plaice, etc., give four fillets. Round fish like cod, or bigger flat fish like turbot, may be cut into fillets or steaks.

## Financière
A garnish including truffles and cocks' combs which, as the name suggests, is highly expensive; for meat and poultry.

## Fines herbes
A mixture of chopped herbs such as thyme, marjoram, parsley, chervil, for making omelets, or herb butter, or adding to forcemeats; may also be simply chopped parsley.

## Finnan haddock
see Haddock

## Flageolet
see Bean

## Flaky pastry
see Pastry

## Flamber
To pour flaming spirit or fortified wine over food with the dual purpose of improving its flavour and burning the alcohol out of the liquor. The dish is usually meat or game (but may be a sweet) and the food is partly or wholly cooked before flaming.

## Flan
A shallow pastry case for either sweet or savoury filling, usually baked blind for filling later, but some fillings (plums, apples and other stone fruit, and some savouries) may be placed in the pastry before baking. The pastry is usually shortcrust. Savoury fillings include meats, fish or cheese mixtures.

## Flapjack
A mixture of rolled oats and brown sugar bound together with butter and baked in a shallow tin; cut into fingers before it cools.

## Fleurons
Puff pastry (or trimmings) rolled out very thin, brushed with beaten egg and cut into small crescent-shaped pieces and baked. Served with fish dishes in which the fish has a rich coating sauce.

## Flitch
A side of bacon. This is half a bacon pig minus the head, hind legs (hams), shoulders and forelegs and after the chine bone has been taken out.

## Florentine
1. A dish served with spinach, in leaf or purée form, either as a garnish or accompaniment.

**2.** An old-fashioned term for a shallow fruit pie with a highly ornamented flaky or puff pastry covering.

**3.** A chocolate-coated, very thin biscuit containing dried fruit and nuts; the chocolate has a characteristic wavy, combed line.

# Flounder
Flat fish common in the shallow, sandy shores round Britain; looks like plaice but has a light brown top and a creamy-white underside. Good, sweet flesh if eaten soon after being caught, but is bony.

# Flour
Cereal grain which has been milled to a powder. Wheat is the most commonly used in ordinary bread and for cooking purposes, the bran, or outer husk, being removed in the milling. Rye is also milled for a number of purposes. It is possible to buy many different types of flour ranging from finest white to wholemeal, which still retains some of the bran, an important roughage material; mills grinding by stone rather than the modern steel rollers can offer a range of flours which include a proportion of bran.

# Fluid ounce
see **Measures**

# Flummery
A Welsh dish in which sugar, cream and sherry are added to an oatmeal jelly.

# Foie gras
The livers of force-fed geese, which may attain a size of 3 or 4 lb weight. Périgueux, Stras-bourg and Toulouse are renowned for their foie gras, which are used mainly for terrines and pâtés.

# Foil
see **Aluminium Foil**

# Fondant
Sugar and water are boiled to 238–240°F, the syrup worked on a flat surface with a wooden spatula until stiff and white, then hand-kneaded until it becomes smooth. May be diluted with a thick syrup for use as an icing (although ready-made fondant powder now may be bought in the shops) or can be used as a chocolate cream centre, flavouring being added in both cases.

# Fonds blanc and Fonds brun
White stock or brown stock. The former is used for things like soups, suprêmes or blanquettes and is made by blanching white meat and bones (veal, etc.) and simmering them with vegetables. For the latter use beef or veal bones, browning them in a little fat before adding the liquid and browned vegetables. The *fonds brun* or brown stock makes braises, ragoûts or *demi-glace*.

# Fondue
**1.** Literally means 'melted'. A Swiss dish in which Gruyère or Emmenthal cheese is melted in a special pot with white wine, kirsch and pepper. Guests around the table spear a piece of bread with a long fork and dip it into the *fondue*, and eat it piping hot. The pot is usually kept hot at the table over a spirit lamp.

**2.** *Fondue bourguignonne* consists of cubes of fillet steak cooked by the guests themselves in a pot of hot oil set over a burner in the middle of the table. The pieces of meat are speared on a long fork for cooking, then dipped in one of a selection of sauces ranged round the burner. They are then transferred to the guest's plate before being eaten with another fork.

**3.** *Fondue* is also the name given to vegetables cooked slowly in butter until they are reduced to a purée.

## Fool

A mixture of one part of partly whipped cream with two parts of sweetened fruit purée such as strawberry (uncooked) or gooseberry (cooked). Served with a sweet biscuit, generally in a glass or coupe.

## Forcemeat
see **Stuffing**

## Fowl

A general term for all eating birds, cock or hen, from the young chicken up to the old boiling fowl, but generally used in connection with the older bird.

## Frangipane

**1.** A pastry cream with almond flavouring.
**2.** A type of cake mixture which is rich and has a good deal of ground almond, used for gâteaux and pâtisseries.

## Frankfurter

A German sausage used in the U.S.A. as a hot dog or served on the Continent with choucroute. Light brown in colour, 4 in or more in length, of finely ground pork, lightly smoked. Cooked by grilling or poaching.

## Frappé

French term applied to iced liquids, creams and fruit sweets.

## Freezer

**1.** A machine for making ices. This may be a wooden bucket with a metal container and a dasher; the space between the bucket and the container is filled with ice and freezing salt, the mixture to be frozen is poured into the container and churned with the dasher until frozen. Alternatively it may be an electric churn which is placed in the freezing compartment of the refrigerator for freezing.
**2.** A cold cabinet for deep freezing fresh and cooked foods to preserve them. To freeze foods successfully it must be possible to achieve a temperature of $-12°F$ for freezing-in and to maintain $32°F$ for storage.

## French dressing

A dressing for salads usually consisting of 3 parts salad oil, 1 part wine vinegar (lemon juice may be used), salt, freshly ground pepper and perhaps mustard; must be shaken or stirred well before use.

## Fricadelle

Small balls of raw meat (or cooked leftovers) fried and possibly served with a sauce.

## Fricandeau

A special piece of fillet cut from a leg of veal, usually braised and served with a traditional garnish, such as purée of sorrel.

## Fricassée

Previously cooked meat which has been warmed up (réchauffé) and served with a white sauce, eg. chicken à la King, or creamed chicken. Usually served with boiled rice as accompaniment.

## Fritter

Slices or pieces of fruit or other foods dipped in fritter batter and fried in deep fat, eg. apple or banana fritters. See also **Kromeski** and **Beignet**.

## Frog

The legs and sometimes the back of the edible green frog known as *Rana esculenta* are eaten extensively in France, where they are regarded as a delicacy. They are usually grilled or fried, but may also be in a fricassée, their tender meat usually flavoured with garlic, onion, etc. In the U.S.A. a different variety of frog is eaten.

## Frosting
see **Icing**

## Frumenty

A breakfast cereal or sweet dish made to an old English country recipe. The basis of the food is whole wheat, which is 'creed', or soaked in cold water and then cooked slowly until it has the consistency of a jelly-like porridge. This is enriched with milk and possibly cream and egg yolks; once spices and honey were also added to make it more tasty. Regarded as rich in vitamins A and B.

## Frying

This is one of the main processes in cookery. It consists of three main types:
*Dry frying* This is done in a thick pan and, despite the term 'dry', the bottom of the pan should have just enough fat to cover it. The pan should be well heated and the food to be fried, mostly cuts such as steaks, cutlets or chops, should be cooked at full heat.
*Shallow frying* The pan should contain fat to a depth of $\frac{1}{4}-\frac{3}{4}$ in, depending on the food to be fried. Used mostly for fish, eggs, fishcakes and crumbed cutlets, the fat should reach halfway up the side of

what is being fried so that it will be evenly browned.

*Deep fat frying* The size and depth of the pan may vary but basically the fat must be deep enough to cover completely what is being fried. The fat should be hot enough to prevent food remaining greasy, ie. above 340°F. Oil must never be heated above 375°F, and for sunflower oil and some commercially prepared fats (eg. Spry, Cookeen) 360°F is the highest recommended temperature. Oil should never be allowed to haze. Some foods, like fried potatoes, are cooked at a lower temperature first and then returned to the fat when it has been heated up again for browning. All deep fried foods should be placed on absorbent paper or drained in some way. The fat or oil may be strained and reused.

## Fudge
A sweetmeat made by boiling a syrup of sugar, milk, butter and flavouring (chocolate, vanilla, etc.) to 240°F. At that temperature it would form a soft ball if dropped into water. The mixture is given a fine graining by being beaten to a thick cream and poured into a shallow tin to cool. It is cut into small squares when cool.

## Fumet
Fumet in modern cookery is generally taken to mean a fish stock that has been well-reduced, but in fact it really means the essence of meat or game as well as fish.

## Galantine
A cold dish which may be made of veal, chicken or duck, boned and spread with various farces. It is poached, roasted or braised and then lightly pressed and coated with chaudfroid or aspic. May be of forcemeat alone, and is often rolled tightly in a cloth for cooking.

## Galette
A flat, round cake of flaky pastry. *Galette des rois* (made in France for Epiphany) is of rich yeast pastry and contains a hidden bean, the finder of which becomes King for the evening. By extension, a round flat cake of vegetables, etc.

## Game
The term is applied to all wild animals and birds protected by law. Rabbit and pigeon are not protected, but are hunted in the same way and for convenience are sold on the same counter and often prepared like game. The open seasons during which game may be shot, are as follows:

August 12—December 10—Grouse and black game.
September 1—February 1—Partridge.
September 1—February 20—Teal, widgeon.
October 1—January 31—Capercailzie, woodcock.
October 1—February 1—

Pheasant.
Late June to January—Red, roe and fallow deer.
Late June to late September—Buck venison.
Rabbits are at their best from September to February, pigeons from March to October and hares from August to February. (The dates given here may vary from time to time; they may also be different in Scotland.)

## Game chip
see **Chip**

## Gammon
The cured foreleg of a pig smoked or green; the hindleg, provides the ham. See also **Bacon**.

## Garbure
A thick vegetable soup or purée made in the region of Béarn in France.

## Garlic
(*Allium sativum*)
A very pungent, onion-like root consisting of 6–8 sections called cloves. Dried like an onion, has a white root and is so strong that it will spoil the flavour of many dishes unless used sparingly; said to be very wholesome.

## Garnish
A trimming which adds to the flavour as well as the appearance of a dish and is therefore important from a culinary point of view. It is often the garnish that gives its name to the dish, eg. *parisienne,* meaning the garnish is of cream sauce with the small mushrooms known as *champignons de Paris*.

## Gazpacho
A traditional, heavily flavoured Spanish soup, usually served ice cold. Made of onion, tomatoes and cucumber with a strong dose of garlic, it is sometimes thickened with white breadcrumbs soaked in olive oil.

## Gâteau
A rich cake, usually pastry based with a heavy cream filling and served as a dessert. May also be applied to a very rich, iced cake.

## Gaufre
see **Waffle**

## Gaufrette
A French wafer biscuit; the name comes from the pattern on it, a gauffering iron being one used to stamp patterns on velvet.

## Gefillte fish
see **Carp**

## Gelatine
A substance used in cookery as a setting agent. It is obtained from animal or fish bones or tissues by a process of prolonged boiling and is usually sold in leaf or powder form. A good quality should always be

used, the quantities needed usually being shown in recipes. See also **Isinglass.**

## Genoese

A type of whisked sponge in which soft, creamed butter is added to the whisked sugar and egg mixture with the flour. Victoria sponge is a type of Genoese. Genoese is widely used in continental *pâtisseries,* particularly in France.

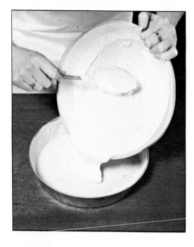

## Ghee

A fat used in Indian cooking; looks like oil but in fact is butter made from buffalo milk and then clarified.

## Gherkin

A miniature cucumber, the best being about 1½ in long grown for pickling and used in cocktail savouries and garnishes.

## Gibelotte

Rabbit, bacon and onions combined in a savoury stew.

## Giblets

The general term for the edible internal parts of poultry, that is the liver, heart, gizzard and neck. With the exception of the liver, the giblets make a good stock for gravy or soup; the stock is improved if the feet are added. Giblets should be well washed before cooking, and the gizzard divested of the thick membrane with grit in it. The feet should be scalded and the outer skin removed. The gall bladder should be carefully removed from the liver without being broken open; the liver is generally used for stuffings or savouries.

## Gigot

The French name (also used in Scotland) for a leg of mutton or lamb.

## Gill

see **Measures**

## Gin

A spirit distilled from grain and flavoured with juniper berries. A corruption of the word *genièvre,* French for juniper. Geneva, another name for gin, is also a corruption of the original word. Originally gin was distilled in Holland and was known as Hollands. Next London became the centre and nowadays it is made all over the world, although much is still called London gin. The base of many aperitifs, its smooth, dry flavour goes well with lemon, tonic water, bitters, etc. Damson or sloe gin may be made at home by infusing berries in gin.

## Ginger

Ginger comes from the rhizome of the plant of the same name and is grated or ground as a flavouring for curries, sauces or chutnies, the Jamaican dried white being the most highly regarded. It may also be bought as stem ginger, preserved in syrup, or crystallised for serving as a dessert. At certain times of the year Britain imports green ginger (the fresh root) from the east.

## Gingerbread
Some parts of northern England still use this old name for ginger cake.

## Girdle
see **Griddle**

## Glacé
French, meaning glazed, or may also be applied to iced dishes. Fruits are said to be *glacé* when they are covered with a syrup which has been boiled to the point at which it will harden when cooled. See also **Syrup** and **Icing**.

## Glaze
1. A strong gravy or bone stock boiled and reduced to a brown syrup which is clear and sets firm on cooling. A mock glaze may be made by stiffening the stock with gelatine. The glaze, or mock glaze, is used to brush over meat, galantines, cold tongues, etc., to improve their appearance. Glaze will also add flavour to a sauce or gravy.
2. Fruit flans, cakes and pastries are glazed by brushing them with a glaze made from red currant jelly or apricot jam.

Used as a verb the word means to make shiny by using a glaze similar to those already mentioned, or with water and sugar, or egg or milk.

## Globe artichoke
see **Artichoke**

## Glucose
Powdered glucose is now well-known medicinally and is made from carbohydrates; it is also called dextrose or grape sugar. A clear syrup form is used in cookery, known as American corn syrup (it can be made from maize or any starch). This is of value in making confectionery since it does not crystallise and will prevent a sugar syrup from graining when it boils.

## Gluten
The strength of a flour depends on the amount of a substance called gluten, which is in the grain of wheat, left in it after milling. It can be given a high gluten content (called springs) by certain processes; this sort of flour is preferred by bakers for making bread because it produces a good elastic dough, and is called 'strong' flour.

## Glycerine

A syrupy liquid used in some forms of royal icing, or in commercially made cakes to keep them moist.

## Gnocchi

Although not strictly a pasta, gnocchi are usually referred to under this heading. There are three main sorts:

*Gnocchi romana* are made with a maize meal called *polenta* (semolina may serve as a substitute), cooked in water and flavoured with cheese.

*French gnocchi* are made with choux pastry, with a cheese flavouring.

*Potato gnocchi* are made from potato mixed with butter, flour and egg. The two first-named are usually served as a separate course with a sauce, whereas potato gnocchi are an accompaniment.

## Goose

Before the turkey was introduced to Britain, roast goose was the dish with which great feast days like Christmas, Michaelmas and harvest time were celebrated. Roast goose should be accompanied by apple sauce and have a stuffing of sage and onion. The meat is rich and tasty.

## Gooseberry

Green gooseberries are one of the most useful and delicious of summer fruits, and make ideal preserves and fools. They may be found from late May or early June to August. There are also red and amber coloured varieties, and all varieties may be cooked or preserved; an ideal dish is made of gooseberries poached with elder flowers, chilled and served with cream.

## Gorgonzola

A blue cheese, made in Italy.

## Goujon

See **Gudgeon**

## Goulash or Gulyas

A Hungarian stew, highly seasoned, usually with paprika and certainly with a large quantity of onions; can be made with veal, beef or lamb.

## Graham flour or bread

A coarse wholemeal flour or bread named in honour of an American dietitian: it is the American equivalent of the Grant Loaf, or granary loaf.

## Graining

When sugar syrup is boiled beyond a temperature of about 245–250°F, it forms small crystals if stirred or agitated in any way. A small quantity of cream of tarter or liquid glucose added to the syrup will delay or stop this graining, or 'cut the grain', as it is called.

## Grant (or Granary) loaf

A loaf of coarse wholemeal bread which may be made at home by mixing yeast, flour and liquid together and putting the mixture straight into the baking tin to rise; it is then baked. The recipe, which eliminates the sponging and proving usually carried out, gets its name from its inventor, Doris Grant. See also **Bread.**

# Grape
The fruit of the vine, used for wine-making and as a dessert. Vines are cultivated in the warmer parts of Europe and other parts of the world. In Britain they are often grown under glass. Different sorts of grapes are grown for different purposes and many are dried as raisins, currants and sultanas.

# Grapefruit
A large citrus fruit with a very distinctive flavour that allows it to be used either as a starter or dessert in a meal. The heavier a grapefruit is compared with its size the more juice it is likely to contain. See **Shaddock,** of which the grapefruit is an improved strain.

# Gratin, Au Gratin or Gratiner
The verb *gratiner* means to brown the surface of a dish with crumbs, butter and perhaps cheese as well. Cooked food coated with a cheese sauce and browned quickly (eg. cauliflower au gratin). Fish may be cooked *au gratin* by covering it with a béchamel or thick white sauce, then browned crumbs and grated cheese (or butter) and baking it. The sauce becomes of a flowing consistency when the juices of the fish mix with it. A fireproof dish with handles on each end is called a *gratin* dish.

# Gravy
Because they are heavier than fat, the juices which flow out of a piece of meat or poultry while it is roasting sink to the bottom of the roasting tin and may easily be recovered by pouring off the liquid fat above them. They may then be diluted with stock, thickened and perhaps coloured according to the dish. Normally served in a sauce boat.

# Grayling
A freshwater fish not sold commercially; similar to a trout in appearance and size.

# Greengage
A fruit of the plum family, dark green in colour, round but slightly flat at the stalk end. The flesh, which is honey sweet and with a distinctive scent, is gold as it becomes ripe. It may be distinguished from the greengage plum, which is a similar fruit, by its round, not oval stone.

# Grenadin
A small round, about 1 in thick, cut from a leg of veal and cooked in the same way as a fricandeau.

## Grey mullet
See **Mullet**

## Griddle (or Girdle)
A thick iron plate used on top of the cooker for baking soda bread, oatcakes and scones. Some have a handle in the shape of a half-hoop.

## Grilling
One of the most important methods of cooking, in which food (particularly steaks, chops, etc.) is subjected to the radiant heat of electric or gas grills, or outdoor barbecue charcoal fires. Spit roasting is often done under a grill.

## Grilse
Grilse are small **Salmon** that have returned to their rivers after being down to the sea for the first time.

## Grissini
Italian bread sticks, long, slim and of a rusk-like, crisp nature, usually put on the table in tumblers.

## Groats
Another name for oatmeal.

## Groundnut oil
See **Oil**

## Ground rice
See **Rice**

## Grouse
A small game bird found on the heathery moors, particularly in Yorkshire and Scotland. It feeds on the tips of the heather. In season from 12 August to 10 December. Grouse should be hung before roasting. Serve with browned crumbs, game chips, strong gravy and red currant jelly.

## Gruel
Oats, barley or other meal made into a thin porridge; once highly regarded for invalids. In Victorian times it was also served in the workhouse.

## Gruyère
A hard cheese from Switzerland, one of the most valued in cookery. Like Emmenthal, a similar Swiss cheese, it has characteristic large holes, although those of Gruyère are the larger; on being cut, these should be moist. Gruyère comes from rich cow's milk and is traditionally used in a fondue. Mixed with Parmesan, it is ideal in a *gratin* or mornay sauce.

## Guava
Small fruit from the tropics, the size of a small apple and with an acid but not unpleasant flavour. Has pulpy red flesh and yellow rind. May be bought canned or fresh.

## Gudgeon
Small, freshwater fish cooked like a whitebait, but rarely seen nowadays. The French borrowed its name to describe small strips of sole or plaice, fried, as being cooked *en goujons*.

61

## Guinea fowl

The name given eventually to an African bird introduced into England in the first half of the 16th century, when it was called 'turkie-henne'. About the size of a large pheasant, it has similar-tasting flesh, but is a domestic bird, dark grey with white spots and dark flesh.

## Gull's egg

The egg of the gull, usually bought ready hard-boiled from the fishmonger, is in season for only a few weeks in late April and early May. It became popular after the taking of plovers' eggs was prohibited by law. The gull's egg, served as a starter with brown bread and butter and rock salt from a grinder, has a taste which is similar to but not quite as delicate as that of the plover.

## Gulyas

See **Goulash**

## Gurnet

A fish found off the Cornish coast. It is spiny and bony, and may be red or grey, like the mullet.

## Hachis

Meat, herbs, etc., minced or chopped and then mixed; used in forcemeats.

## Haddock

A fish weighing 1½–6 lb, round, and rated one of the best white fish; has a black smudge behind each gill which is called St. Peter's Mark, a grey skin and a black line running down each side.

Sold fresh or smoked. Fresh haddock, because of its firm white flesh, lends itself to cooking in numerous ways, including whole with a stuffing of forcemeat and herbs, roasted like a joint of meat with gravy from the juices, poached with a sauce, or fried. The smoked haddock, which originated in the village of Findon, or Finnon, near Aberdeen, ranges from cured fillets of the large fish down to small whole fish known as smokies.

## Haggis

Haggis is as Scottish as bagpipes and tartans, but as well

as being traditional is also a good warming dish for a cold day. It is a rich forcemeat of liver, heart and tongue with oatmeal, stuffed into small bags made from the paunch of a sheep and boiled gently for 2–3 hours before being sold in the shop. At home a haggis should be simmered for another hour. Traditionally it is served hot on a napkin, the skin split and the stuffing spooned out, with boiled potatoes and mashed turnips.

## Hake
A large white fish not unlike a cod in appearance and weight, but with a rough grey skin. Mostly found off the coasts of south-west England, it is popular and its white, easily digestible flesh is good for creams and mousses.

## Halibut
A huge type of flat fish which, because it might weigh anything up to 100 lb, is sold by the piece for boiling or in steaks for grilling. Has a high food value but lacks the delicate flavour of turbot; its firm white flesh is somewhat coarse.

## Halva
A confectionery made in the Middle East with sugar, butter, nuts and ground sesame seed or semolina, and a saffron or rosewater flavouring. Also made in India.

## Ham
The cured hind leg of a bacon pig. There are many sorts of hams, some smoked, some just cured, the best known of the latter being the English York Ham, large and with a very delicate flavour. Bradenhams,

from Norfolk, and imported Virginia hams, are special cures. Less expensive than these and smaller are the 10–12 lb smoked hams from Denmark and Ireland, while many Continental countries have their specialities (Parma, Bayonne, Prague) sliced thin and eaten without cooking See also **Bacon.**

## Hamburgers
Minced raw beef shaped into individual round cakes and dry-fried in the pan. Fried onion is the normal accompaniment.

## Hare
Highly flavoured game, excellent eating open season September to end of January. Of the two varieties brown hare is better than the blue, or mountain, hare. A hare is at its best up to 2 years old; the French call a young leveret up to 3 months a *financier,* up to 6 months a *trois-quarts* and at 1 year a *capucin,* or *lièvre pit.* Young hare should be sautéd or roasted, but older hares need

63

long, slow cooking, such as jugging, in stock or wine. If freshly killed a hare should be hung, head downwards, for 8–12 days so that the blood can collect in the rib cage, and paunched (insides removed) after 4 days. Care must be taken not to break the membrane across the rib cage until a container is ready to catch the blood, which is used in the cooking. The blood is kept in the refrigerator while the hare is marinating prior to cooking, and then used to thicken the sauce.

# Haricot
1. A bean, usually dried. See also **Bean**.
2. A brown stew of mutton, carrots and onions. See also **Navarin**.

# Hâtelet
See **Attelette**

# Hazelnut
Sometimes called a Barcelona, small, round and grown on the hazel tree. The kernels of the nuts are generally toasted or lightly baked before use, making it easy to remove their skins. Used ground, or whole, in making confectionery or cakes.

# Heart
Edible offal, the best being that of the sheep; usually stuffed with a good herb stuffing and braised until tender.

# Herbs
Herbs include a wide range of plants used in flavouring, but they must be treated with respect since many are strong and pungent in flavour and some enhance certain foods more than others. The main herbs are **Basil, Bay, Chives, Dill, Fennel, Marjoram, Mint, Parsley, Rosemary, Savory, Tarragon.** See also **Fines Herbes** and appendix chart.

# Herring
One of the commonest fish round England's shores, 7–10 inches long, silvery in colour. Herrings move round the coast in shoals, reaching the Great Yarmouth area of the east by about October after taking 6–7 months to travel from the northwest part of the British Isles. May be smoked and eaten as kippers or bloaters, or cooked fresh, when they should be eaten as soon as possible after being caught, before the delicate flesh becomes too oily.

# Hip
The hip is the fruit of the wild (dog) rose, known as *Rosa canina,* which contains Vitamin C. A pleasant tasting jelly may be made from it which, like red currant jelly, can be served with game or meat. An apple is needed when making jelly to supplement pectin in the hip. Also makes an excellent syrup for drinking.

# Hock
A German wine, white, originally from Hochheim-on-Main but now the name is applied to most Rhine wines, which are distinguished by their tall brown bottles.

# Hollandaise
1. A method of cooking (*à la hollandaise*).
2. A rich Dutch or Holland sauce made from butter and eggs and

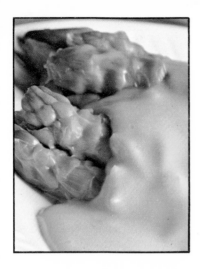

usually served with vegetables, such as asparagus, or fish.

# Hominy

Maize which has been ground into a meal resembling a coarse semolina. In the past it was extensively used for making croquettes and cream sweets.

# Homogenise

Homogenised liquid is that which has been emulsified. Milk which has been homogenised (its fat particles broken up and dispersed) is more digestible than ordinary milk.

# Honey

A natural, liquid form of sugar which bees prepare. The flavour depends on where the bees have fed, such as in heather, lime, or clover. Probably the earliest form of sweetening; may be clear or thick (containing some wax) or still in the comb when purchased.

# Hors d'oeuvre

Small dishes aimed at whetting the appetite; these form the introduction to a meal, particularly lunch. Originally cold hors d'oeuvre were served with lunch and hot with dinner, but both may now be served at the same time. The dishes chosen should be tempting, light and delicious, perhaps a collection of piquant salads such as anchovy fillets, egg mayonnaise, Russian salad, salami, *crudités* (raw vegetables) and spiced fish.

# Horseradish

A condiment made by grating the root of the *Cochlearia armoracia* plant. The hot, astringent taste is a perfect complement to roast beef. May be mixed with some cream which has been lightly whipped to make a horseradish sauce, or for cold beef or salads, may simply be grated over it.

# Hot cross bun

Traditional Good Friday bun, made of yeast dough with currants and possibly candied peel. The top is marked with a cross.

# Hot dog

American name for a frankfurter sausage, boiled or grilled and served hot with mustard inside a long soft bread roll.

# Hot-pot

A traditional dish in the Midlands and north of England, originally cooked in a special earthenware dish not often seen nowadays. The famous Lancashire hot-pot consists of layers of meat, mushrooms and oysters under a top layer of potatoes. The dish is cooked without a lid so as to allow the potato to brown.

# Hurt

See **Bilberry**

## Iberian moss
See **Carrageen**

## Ices
A firm mass of frozen, sweetened liquid, which might be a light syrup flavoured with, say, orange or lemon, or a custard, or a mixture of egg yolks and cream. A frozen mass can be achieved in the deep freeze or refrigerator ice tray, but this lacks the smooth and light texture obtained by freezing while the mixture is being churned in an ice cream freezer. Care must be taken to follow the sugar content given in the recipe, since too little sugar will produce a flavourless and hard ice cream. Too much sugar will stop it freezing.

## Icing
A coating made mainly with sugar for decorating cakes. The best-known types of icing are:
*Butter Icing* (for plain cakes) Icing sugar creamed with butter and appropriate flavour like orange, chocolate, etc.
*Fondant* (for light cakes like Genoese) Sugar, water and cream of tartar boiled to 240°F and worked with spatula until it becomes a firm and white fondant. Before being used it is reduced to a creamy consistency with a little sugar syrup, flavoured and slightly warmed.
*Glacé* Flavouring and syrup or water mixed with icing sugar to a creamy consistency. Can be used as substitute for fondant if made with syrup.

*Royal Icing* (For wedding, birthday cakes etc.) Egg white is added to icing sugar to produce the hard white effect typical of these cakes. Certain pastries in France are given a crisp finish by addition of a small quantity of soft royal icing spread on them before baking.
*Frosting* (American-style icing) Made by whisking sugar and egg white together over heat, or by whisking egg whites and beating together with sugar made into a syrup and boiled to 240°F, until a soft but crisp icing is obtained.

## Icing sugar
See **Sugar**

## Indian corn
Better known in England as sweet corn. Can be eaten on the cob, creamed, or plain. Cobs are up to 8 in long and grow in a green husk on a plant about 6 ft high with pointed green leaves. The kernels provide the raw material for maize, hominy, polenta and cornflour when dried, but are soft and milky when cooked as green corn.

## Ink fish
See **Octopus**

## Irish stew
Mutton and onion stewed very slowly with potatoes to form a white stew. The gravy is thickened slightly by the potatoes breaking up.

## Isinglass
A gelatine preparation which may be substituted for other gelatines when milk and meat products cannot be used together for religious reasons. Isinglass comes from dried fish bladder, particularly that of a sturgeon.

## Jam
Fresh fruit and sugar mixed and boiled until the pectin content of the fruit produces a confection that will set on cooling. This is a popular method of preserving fruit. Jam differs from conserve in that the fruit usually becomes pulped in the former, whereas in the latter it remains whole, in heavy syrup.

## Jamaican pepper
See **Allspice**

## Jardinière (à la)
Beans, peas, carrots, turnips and other fresh vegetables cooked and served separately around a dish as a garnish. They are usually shaped or diced.

## Jelly
A liquid set firm, naturally or by the introduction of gelatine; may be sweet or savoury. A good stock made from marrow bones may set itself when cold. Such a stock may be clarified and made into aspic. If a stiff jelly is required, for instance for moulding, a small amount of gelatine may be added. A sweet jelly may be made with the stock from a calf's foot, but would normally be prepared from commercial gelatine. A jelly fruit preserve is made by boiling the juice of the fruit with sugar until it will set.

## Jelly bag
A device for clarifying jellies through felt or coarse wool material. Special stands for hanging the bags are available.

## Jersey wonder
A Jersey island speciality made from flour, eggs and butter mixed into a rich dough, shaped like knots and fried in deep fat until golden-brown, then served hot with a fruit sauce.

## Jerusalem artichoke
See **Artichoke**

## John Dory
A flat fish caught off the south-west coasts of England. Has a large, ugly head for its size, making its firm white flesh, which has a delicate taste, somewhat expensive.

## Juggery
An Indian dessert. A European imitation can be made with tapioca, black treacle, sugar, cream and coconut.

## Julienne
A garnish in which vegetables must be cut into shreds about $1\frac{1}{2}$ in long. The name is also applied to this method of cutting, and to a clear vegetable soup made from a consommé with julienne vegetables added.

## Jumble
A thin wafer biscuit, curled or rolled; a brandy snap.

## Juniper
A dark purplish berry with a spicy, pungent taste from a small evergreen bush not unlike a fir tree. Used fresh or dried in marinades for game; also used medicinally and in the making of gin.

## Junket
A curd made by setting milk with rennet.

## Jus
French name for juices from meat (gravy) or fruit.

## Kabab
See **Kebab**

## Kale
A winter vegetable which is cooked like cabbage and is a member of the same family (*Brassica*) as the cabbage. Has crispy green curled leaves.

## Kangaroo
Kangaroo (or wallaby) tail soup is an Australian delicacy exported in cans.

## Kebab
A form of Middle East cookery in which pieces of meat are skewered, then roasted or grilled. The meat is usually lamb, and bay leaves and onion slices are held on the kebab skewers with the meat.

## Kedgeree
Fish and rice mixed together, possibly with cream and eggs added for moistening. Originally an Indian dish.

## Ketchup
A bottled sauce in which one flavour is predominant against a spicy background. Tomato ketchup, for instance, is made of tomato purée with vinegar and spices, mushroom ketchup from the juice of mushrooms steeped in vinegar, with spices.

## Kid
A young goat, which should not be more than four months old; a delicacy when roasted.

## Kidney
See **Offal**. One of the edible internal parts of an animal.
*Lamb's kidney* Regarded as the best, may be grilled or sautéd.
*Calf's kidney* Has a delicate flavour sautéd or braised, whole or sliced.
*Pig's kidney* Like lamb's kidney but bigger and with a much stronger flavour; used more in stuffings or pâtés.
*Ox kidney* Large, strongly flavoured and tough; used more in steak and kidney pudding or pie.

## Kipper
A herring that has been kippered, ie. split, salted and then smoked.

## Kirsch
The best kirsch is a liqueur distilled in the Alsace region of France and the Black Forest of Germany, from fermented wild cherries. Its flavour goes well with fruit, particularly pineapple, and it is used in cream sweets and soufflés.

## Kissel
See **Röd Gröd**

## Kneading
When a dough has been made from flour, yeast, water, etc., it is turned out on to a floured board, the edge lifted over to the centre and the whole 'kneaded' with the knuckles, which push it outwards. One of the most important parts of bread-making kneading is repeated numerous times either by hand or with an electric mixer bread-hook to develop the gluten in the dough.

## Knives
Kitchen knives follow certain patterns or shapes, should be of good quality steel and kept well sharpened and clean. They are usually described with the length of the blade. Main types are:
*Chopping knife* Either large or medium, used for all purposes, with a firm blade and fairly heavy.
*Filleting knife* A blade about six in long, flexible, narrow and pointed, for filleting fish, slices of chicken, etc.
*Vegetable knife* Small knife in different blade sizes for cutting vegetables.

69

*Fruit or vegetable knife* Made of stainless steel since carbon steels stain some fruit or vegetables. A serrated edge is helpful.

*Palette knife* Round-bladed, flexible, with no cutting edge; used for turning food or lifting it.

# Kohlrabi

A root vegetable resembling a turnip, cooked and served like a swede. Has blue-green leaves.

# Kromeski

Chicken, game or veal cut into small pieces, creamed and wrapped in thin rashers of bacon, dipped in fritter batter and deep-fried. May be served as main course or savoury.

# Kulich

A Russian Easter cake made of rich dough like brioche. It is baked in tall, thin tins and sliced across so that the top can be replaced if not eaten all at once. The top is iced and covered with hundreds and thousands.

# Kümmel

A liqueur with the flavour of cummin or caraway seeds.

# Kumquat

Small citrus fruit, often preserved whole in syrup and bottled.

# Lactic acid

Acid obtained from sour milk. See also **Pasteurise, Milk.**

# Lamb

Young sheep up to the age of eight months. See diagram in appendix.

# Lamb's lettuce

See **Corn Salad**

# Lamprey

A sea fish resembling an eel which, like salmon, spawns in certain rivers. It fastens itself on to wood, stone or other objects under water, including other fish, which it eats. Can be stewed, baked or made into a pie. In the Middle Ages lampreys were a great delicacy and were caught in large quantities in the earlier part of the year, particularly in the River Severn. Legend has it that a surfeit of lampreys killed Henry I; this may have been due to their soft flesh being highly indigestible.

# Langouste

See **Crawfish**

# Langue de chat

A biscuit which is thin and flat like a cat's tongue, served as petit four or with ices and cream sweets. May be of plain chocolate in confectionery, or a sponge biscuit mixture, straw coloured in the centre and browned round the edges when baked.

## Lard

Fat of a pig which has been rendered down, sometimes flavoured with rosemary, but should be odourless and white. Used for frying (is the best after oil) or for shortening.

## Larding

Certain cuts of meat, like fillet of beef or veal, which have almost no fat of their own are given additional fat by a process called larding. This consists of sewing pieces of fat (see **Lardons**) on to them with a larding needle.

## Lardon

Specially cured larding bacon (without saltpetre) is all fat and is cut into strips, or lardons, about $1\frac{1}{2}$ in long and $\frac{1}{4}$ in wide and thick, for the process of larding. Pork fat is a good substitute when larding bacon cannot be obtained, although many delicatessens sell a Polish variety called Spik (German Speck).

## Lasagne

One of the many varieties of Italian pasta: a wide ribbon which may be plain, or *Lasagne verde,* which gets its colour and flavour from spinach. Like other pasta, lasagne may be made easily or it may be bought in packets at the delicatessen. The paste is dried and lightly boiled, then layered with a meat mixture and coated with a cheese sauce, or just cheese, and browned in the oven.

## Laver

Edible seaweed which, after being well washed, is stewed until it becomes a pulp. Lemon juice, salt and pepper and some butter are added and the laver is heated again and eaten either as a vegetable with meat, or as a savoury on hot toast. Often sold ready cooked in seaside towns; both the green (*Ulva latissima*) and purple (*Porphyra laciniata*) varieties are common in the British Isles.

## Leek

(*Allium porrum*)

A long cylindrical-shaped member of the onion family, with a similar but far more subtle flavour than the onion itself. Leeks can be served as a vegetable or used as a flavouring, or served cold with a vinaigrette dressing or mayonnaise in salad. Grown in a trench and blanched to give 4–5 inches of white stem, are best between November and March.

## Lemon

One of the most important citrus fruits for culinary purposes, imported into England all year round, mostly from the Mediterranean. All parts of the lemon are widely used: the pips and pith have a high pectin content, the rind (or zest) and juice are important flavourings; lemon juice often substitutes for vinegar in salad dressings. The lemon is however rarely eaten as a fruit in its own right.

## Lemon balm
See **Balm**

## Lemon sole
See **Sole**

## Lentil
(*Lens esculenta*)
The seed, two to a pod, of a hardy annual which, when dried, looks somewhat like a small split pea and is cooked in a similar fashion, although it belongs to a different family. The German or brown variety and the golden lentil are both sold in England, the latter being smaller and easier to cook; both may be used for soups, purées, Indian dhal, etc., and need long soaking before cooking.

## Lettuce
A vegetable whose crisp green leaves and heart are the almost universal basis for salads, although in some countries they are also cooked. The cabbage, so-called because of its round cabbage shape, and the cos, long, upright and with crisper leaves, are the two best known. Grown in the open during the summer and under glass or imported from October onwards.

## Leveret
Young hare.

## Liaison
A mixture for thickening and binding sauces, gravies and soups. The most common are a roux, kneaded butter or egg yolks and cream.

## Lights
The lungs of an animal, mostly of a bullock. Their name comes from the fact that they are very light in weight.

## Lima bean
See **Bean**

## Lime
(*Citrus limetta*)
A citrus fruit similar to the lemon, grown in the West Indies and imported in small quantities into Britain as whole fruit. Thin skinned and green and mainly used for its juice.

## Ling
Generally dried and salted, ling is a coarse, large cod which must be well soaked before being included in fish stew, etc.

## Liqueur
Alcoholic spirit based on wine or brandy and flavoured with spices, herbs or fruit, usually drunk in tiny glasses after a meal. Most well-known liqueurs are based on closely guarded secret formulae, although their main ingredient might be obvious. See **Benedictine, Cherry Brandy, Crème de Menthe, Curaçao, Drambuie, Kirsch, Kümmel, Maraschino, Noyau.**

## Liver
An offal, to be eaten without being hung, and not overcooked. Is very nutritious and extensively used in cookery in most countries. Calf's liver has the most delicate flavour, and is the most expensive, followed closely by lamb's liver. Both lend themselves ideally to the traditional fried liver and bacon, usually with fried onions. Pig's liver is best for pâtés, terrines and stuffing; ox liver is coarse and strong-tasting and not often used. The liver of geese and other poultry is used for pâtés and specialised dishes. See **Continental Sausages.**

# Lobster

Regarded in England as the best of the shellfish. The average weight is 1–1¼ lb, the shell dark greenish-blue when raw but brilliant red when cooked. Over-large or barnacled lobsters should be avoided. Hen lobsters are prized for their coral, or spawn, used for flavouring and colouring lobster butter for sauces, while the cock has fine, slightly firmer flesh. The season for lobsters round Britain's coasts is from March to October although they are available (and expensive) at other times. For hot lobster dishes the lobster should be live and killed by piercing the brain just before cooking, while freshly boiled lobster is used in cold dishes.

# Loganberry

A summer soft fruit, similar to the raspberry but bigger and more acid. Makes excellent jam, or purée for ice creams or fools.

# Loin

The part of an animal's carcass from the tail to the ribs. A saddle of lamb consists of the two loins still joined together; the same cut in beef is called a baron of beef.

# Lovage

(*Levisticum officinale*)
A perennial herb with a strong flavour of celery. The lovage has a serrated leaf of greenish-grey colour.

## Luting paste

When a pâté is being cooked it is desirable to keep the steam in the terrine; a luting paste made of flour and water is used to seal the lid of the terrine.

## Lychee

A fruit from China, shaped something like a cherry and growing in bunches on a tree, like the cherry. It has a thin shell, easily removed, and the flesh within has a pinky-white colour, the texture of a muscat grape and a very delicate flavour.

Sometimes lychees are dried in the shell, when they look like raisins, but can usually be bought in cans and sometimes fresh.

## Lyonnais

A term meaning that a dish originated in the region of Lyons, in France, noted for its fine onions and potatoes. The region is an important one gastronomically and gave rise to many specialities like *quenelles de brochet, gras double lyonnaise, pâtés,* and sausages.

## Macaroni

One of the best-known types of Italian pasta, in the form of a $\frac{1}{4}$-in diameter tube. Like other pasta, cooked by simmering in water until tender, drained and mixed with a sauce. One of the most popular dishes is macaroni cheese; in Victorian times macaroni figured as a milk pudding.

## Macaroon

A rich, round biscuit made from ground almonds, egg white and sugar. In France, where it originated, the best-known macaroon comes from Nancy.

## Mace

A spice made from the tendrils covering a nutmeg, more delicate in flavour than the nutmeg itself. Ground mace is used with mixed spices in stuffings and vegetable dishes. Blade mace, with the tendrils left whole, is used in béchamel sauce, etc.

## Macédoine

A macédoine of fruit consists of peaches, bananas, pears, etc., sliced up, mixed and covered with a thick syrup. Macédoine of vegetables is usually carrots, potatoes, turnips, etc., diced and mixed with peas or beans and then served cold with mayonnaise, or hot with a white sauce.

## Macerate

To soak or infuse in liquid. Usually used of fresh or glacé fruit soaked in brandy, rum or liqueur.

## Mackerel

A fighting fish with a well-marked blue/silver skin caught off British coasts and in northern waters from May to September. If eaten fresh, the flesh is firm and crisp, but if left more than a few days it becomes tasteless and oily.

74

# Madeira

A wine from the Spanish territory of the same name which may be taken like sherry as an aperitif, or like port, as a dessert wine (the same sort of glasses are used). Varies from dry and pale to rich brown; may also be used in a *demi-glace* or brown sauce to go with a fillet of beef, braised ham or other dishes (*sauce madère*).

# Madeira cake

One of the best-known English cakes, baked from a rich genoese mixture in which the proportion of butter and eggs to flour is high. Traditionally baked with a slice or slices of citron peel placed on the top.

# Madeleine

The English madeleine is a Victoria sponge mixture put into round-topped castle pudding moulds and baked. The cakes are then given a red jam glaze, rolled in shredded coconut and decorated with a glacé cherry each. The French madeleine is a small cake of genoese mixture baked in a small, cockle shell mould.

# Madère

See **Madeira**

# Maid of honour

A type of pastry which originated in Richmond-upon-Thames, Surrey: consists of a rich almond cheesecake baked in a puff pastry case.

# Maigre

A dish that is without meat.

# Maître d'hôtel

1. The person in charge of the restaurant; slightly more than a head waiter, however, since the maître d'hôtel should be experienced in cookery and able to make some dishes at the table, such as steak tartare, steak au poivre, etc.
2. A simple method of preparing or finishing a dish, for instance maître d'hôtel butter is butter mixed with chopped parsley and lemon juice, added as a finishing touch to plain fish or grilled meat.

# Maize

Indian corn kernels; often made into a meal (*polenta*) for bread, scones and pudding. See also **Indian corn, Polenta.**

# Malaga

A Spanish wine that is sweet and heavy. Malaga raisins, very sweet, are made from muscat grapes.

# Mallard

One of the best-known and most frequently caught of game ducks. See also **Duck.**

# Malt

Barley or other grain in which fermentation has changed the starch into sugar; used in distillation and brewing. Bakers make a malt loaf by adding an extract of malt to their dough.

# Mandarin

See **Orange**

# Mandolin

A vegetable slicer: a blade, usually slanted and which can be adjusted for thickness, is set in a rectangle of wood or metal and the vegetable sliced by rubbing it up and down over the blade.

## Mango

A tropical fruit not imported to Europe in any great quantity, and therefore expensive to buy fresh. The fruit varies in colour from rich yellow to olive green with a soft, juicy but stringy pulp and with a sweet and delicate flavour. Mango chutney is well-known in Britain; tinned mangoes are good for cooking but lose much of the flavour of the fresh fruit.

## Maple syrup

The sap of the sugar maple tree, made into maple syrup by boiling and refining, which stops it fermenting. This syrup is a traditional accompaniment to waffles, American pancakes and hot sweets, and is also used for flavouring. The sugar maple or *Acer saccharinum* grows mostly in Canada and the northern United States.

## Maraschino

A liqueur made from the *marasca* or wild black cherry which grows in Dalmatia, Yugoslavia. The seeds as well as the flesh of the fruit are used, giving the liqueur its characteristic nutty taste.

## Marc

An eau-de-vie made from the pressings or crushed pulp of grapes pressed for wine.

## Marengo

A classic chicken dish said to have been created hurriedly on the night of June 14, 1800, after Napoleon had fought and defeated the Austrians on the battlefield at Marengo. He ordered his chef, named Dunand, to prepare a celebration meal but because of their position all they could find consisted of a small hen, six crayfish, some eggs, tomatoes and garlic, oil and a frying pan. The worthy and resourceful chef produced a sauté which, with some brandy from the Emperor's flask, brought praise from Napoleon who said, 'You must feed me like this after every battle'.

## Margarine

A cooking fat which may be manufactured from animal fats or vegetable oils, particularly useful for making light pastry or cakes. It can be produced more cheaply than butter. Vegetable margarine is frequently used in place of butter when animal fats have to be excluded from the diet.

## Marinade

A liquid in which meat, fish or poultry is allowed to soak, or marinate, for a certain length of time before being cooked. The process is used extensively in French cookery, the purpose being to help tenderise the food concerned as well as give it extra flavour. The marinade may have various ingredients according to the food concerned, but usually consists of oil, wine, sliced onions and carrots, and various herbs or spices. If it has been boiled and cooled before use it is called a *marinade cuite*, it is otherwise known as a *marinade crue*. Some foods may marinate for days before cooking, others for only a few hours.

## Marinière

A method of cooking mussels or other shellfish with white wine. The term is also used for certain fish dishes which have mussels as a garnish.

## Marjoram
(*Origanum*)
Sweet marjoram is one of the best-known herbs, often used in stuffings for veal or lamb; there are other types of the herb.

## Marmalade
A preserve of citrus fruits, boiled with sugar as for jam.

## Marmelade
Fruit pulp boiled with sugar and reduced to the consistency of a fruit cheese; used as a filling in a flan where the fruit is placed on the uncooked pastry. Some European countries, particularly Spain, make confectionery this way, cutting the marmelade into squares.

## Marrons glacés
Glazed chestnuts. Whole chestnuts are peeled and cooked, then poached for hours in sugar syrup. The strength of the syrup is increased as cooking progresses, the chestnuts becoming semi-clear before they are finally glazed with a specially beaten sugar mixture. This is a complicated confectionery process which makes the finished sweet expensive; it is not recommended for making at home

## Marrow (bone)
The bones, particularly the shank-bones, of a bullock or calf are filled with a marrow which becomes a jelly when cooked. Marrow bones make a delicious savoury served hot with pepper and dry toast.

## Marrow (vegetable)
A vegetable of the gourd family, of which there are numerous sizes and shapes sold under various names in different countries. The flesh of the ordinary marrow is tender if eaten young; may be cooked in many ways, but is best stewed in butter, stuffed or fried in breadcrumbs.

## Marsala
A sweet Sicilian wine, traditionally used for zabaglione; not unlike a Madeira but not as good quality. Mostly used in cooking.

## Marzipan
A thick paste made from ground almonds and sugar; generally used as a base for icing on Christmas, wedding and birthday cakes, or in confectionery.

## Matelote
Denotes fish stewed in wine, usually according to the region where it is made, such as matelote bourguignonne, a fresh water fish stew made with the red wine of Burgundy, or normande, sea fish with white wine and cream.

## Mayonnaise
A sauce for dressing cold meats, salads, etc., made thick and

77

rich by mixing egg yolks and oil and sharpening the taste of this with vinegar (or lemon juice).

## Mead

One of the oldest drinks, brewed extensively in the Middle Ages but now made only rarely in England. It is made from honey-combs after they have been cleared of honey, and flavoured with certain spices and herbs.

## Measures

There are variations in the standard measures used in Britain, the United States and Continental Europe. (See below.)

## Medaillon

Meat (or possibly some other food) cut into small oval or round pieces. See **Tournedos.** Also the name for a round piece of French flan pastry which has been iced and given a marbled effect with chocolate or contrasting colour icing.

## Medlar

A fruit about plum size, brown and with a firm flesh, grown on the medlar tree (*Mespilus germanicus*). Used for medlar jelly, or fruit cheese, or may be eaten raw, but in all cases it must be very ripe.

## Melba

The great chef Escoffier paid his tribute to the singer Dame Nellie Melba with a dessert called Peach Melba: a peach cooked in a vanilla-flavoured syrup and served with ice cream and a purée of fresh raspberries.

## Melon

There are numerous types of this fruit, which is a member of

| British Imperial pint | Cups, etc. | Fluid oz |
|---|---|---|
| $\frac{1}{8}$ pint | 1 sherry glass ($\frac{1}{2}$ gill) | $2\frac{1}{2}$ fl oz |
| — | 1 wineglass ($\frac{3}{4}$ gill) | $3\frac{3}{4}$ fl oz |
| $\frac{1}{4}$ pint | 1 gill | 5 fl oz |
| $\frac{1}{3}$ pint | 1 teacup (approx.) | $6\frac{2}{3}$ fl oz |
| $\frac{1}{2}$ pint (American) | 1 American cup | 8 fl oz |
| $\frac{1}{2}$ pint | 1 British Standard (breakfast) cup | 10 fl oz |
| $\frac{4}{5}$ pint | 1 American pint | 16 fl oz |
| 1 pint | 2 B.S. cups | 20 fl oz |
| $1\frac{1}{2}$ pints | 5-inch diameter pudding basin | — |
| $1\frac{3}{4}$ pints | 1 litre | 35 fl oz |
| 2 pints | 1 quart | — |
| 8 pints | 1 gallon (4 quarts) | — |

Approximate metric equivalents:

1 oz = 28·35 grams (g)
$3\frac{1}{2}$ oz = 100 g
4 oz = 114 g
8 oz = 225 g
1 lb = 450 g
2 lb $3\frac{1}{2}$ oz = 1 kilogram (kg) = 1,000 g

5 fl oz ($\frac{1}{4}$ pint) = $\frac{1}{8}$ litre (l)
1 pint = $\frac{1}{2}$ litre = 570 millilitres (ml)
2 gallons 2 pints = 10 litres
10 centilitres = 1 decilitre (dl)
10 decilitres = 1 litre
10 litres = 1 dekalitre (dkl)

the same family as the cucumber. The most familiar in Britain are:

*Honeydew* A green, rough-skinned fruit, quite large. The flesh has a honey taste and a pale colour. Medium priced. Available after midsummer.
*Cantaloup* With the Charentais, usually the most expensive in Britain. Largish, skin divided into segments and rough-textured. August-September.
*Charentais* Pale-green in colour and available in early summer; comes from the Charente region of France and is small but sweet, with a delicious flavour.
*Spanish water* Yellow skin, sweet flesh, medium to large in size; available in later summer, usually cheap and often called Honeydew despite the differences between the two.
*Watermelon* Better known in hotter climates, but now imported into England: large and round, characterised by green, smooth skin, red flesh and black seeds. Sweet but thin flavour, available in summer.

## Melt
See **Milt**

## Menu
The dishes chosen for a particular meal (rather than the card listing all the dishes available, say, in a restaurant). This structure, or planning, of a meal is important both nutritionally and otherwise. In the past a menu was far more impressive than now, when a three-course lunch and maximum five-course dinner are more fashionable. In the case of the latter the five are usually chosen from hors d'oeuvre, soup, fish, entrée, remove or relevé, sorbet, roast, entremets and dessert.

## Meringue
A mixture of egg white and sugar thought to have been invented in the early 18th century by a Swiss pastrycook named Gasparini. Suisse, cuite and italienne are the three main types:
*Suisse* Two ounces of caster sugar to each egg white, which is stiffly whipped before the sugar is folded in. Used in meringue shells with crème chantilly, or on top of a dessert.
*Cuite* Means cooked, but in fact this meringue is not cooked but has egg whites and sugar whisked together over hot water. This gives a harder meringue than the suisse, used as a base for creams, in petits fours, or for meringue baskets.
*Italienne* Used more by professionals than in the house, this requires a sugar thermometer because lump sugar is made into a syrup and boiled to 260°F before being poured on to whisked egg whites and whisked again. Used in such dishes as baked alaska and in pâtisseries.

## Meunière

Whole fish or fillets to be cooked by this method are floured lightly and fried to a golden-brown colour in foaming butter. They are then removed and set aside and the pan cleaned; more butter is added and when cooked to a nut-brown colour, herbs and lemon juice are added to form a *beurre noisette* which is served over the fish.

## Mignonette

Another name for white pepper which is coarsely ground.

## Milk

A liquid secreted by the mammary glands of animals, that of the cow being the most commonly used in Britain, although some goat's milk is also used. Contains high proportions of protein and fat. Widely used as a drink, and in puddings, sauces and cold sweets. Most of the milk sold in Britain is now first subjected to a heat-treatment, or pasteurised, to destroy harmful bacteria. The lactic acid in such milk is destroyed by pasteurisation and natural souring cannot take place; milk required for home-made curds and cheese must therefore be unpasteurised. For their culinary purposes, pasteurisation makes little difference.

## Mille-feuille

A French pastry made with thin, crispy puff pastry built up in layers with whipped cream and raspberry or strawberry jam or pastry cream, topped with thin fondant or glacé icing and cut into slices. Sometimes known as vanilla slices. Large rings of baked puff pastry built up on one another and the centre filled with cream and fruit is called a gâteau mille-feuille.

## Milt (or Melt)

1. In fish, the soft roe.
2. In meat, the spleen, which once was thought to have the same function as fish roes.

## Mincemeat

Traditional filling for a Christmas mince pie consisting of finely chopped suet, dried fruit, apples, candied peel, almonds, spices and preferably a good lacing of rum or brandy to help it keep.

## Minestra and Minestrone

Minestra is a purely vegetable soup; minestrone is similar but may contain pieces of bacon or ham. Both are Italian and served with Parmesan cheese, although minestra is said to have originated in Spain.

## Mint

A sweet, aromatic herb, very good for mint sauce and general flavouring. Some mints are scented: apple, pineapple and eau-de-cologne, the two latter being particularly good as a tea or for flavouring a fruit or wine cup. Apple mint is a good substitute for sage in a stuffing or for flavouring an apply jelly.

# Mirepoix
Generally used as a base for a braise of meat, or to give flavour to certain sauces, a mirepoix is a mixture of diced root vegetables, sometimes with raw bacon or ham added.

# Mocha
The region of Mocha in Arabia produces a particular variety of coffee bean; by extension anything with a coffee flavouring may be described as 'mocha'.

# Molasses
See Treacle

# Monosodium glutamate
A chemical substance obtained from some food proteins and used to bring out the flavour of certain foods. It is said to decrease certain tastes, for instance the bitter or metallic taste in tomato purée, and increase flavours in foods like sausages, bouillon cubes and meat extracts, as well as canned foods. It has no recognisable flavour.

# Morel
One of the edible fungi, grey to yellow-brown in colour and with a honeycombed, spongy cap. *Morchella esculenta* is probably the commonest of the various varieties of morel. May be found in the hedgerows or woodland clearings in spring, and cooked like mushrooms.

# Morello
A variety of cherry with a tart, acid taste and a semi-translucent, deep red colour. Used for making cherry brandy and for jams; picked in late July and early August.

# Mornay
A béchamel sauce containing cheese (mornay sauce). A dish of egg, vegetable or fish coated with mornay sauce, and then glazed under the grill or in the oven.

# Mortadella
See Continental Sausages

# Morue
The French name for salt cod. The classic ingredient for making a brandade, after it has been well soaked.

# Moselle
A white wine from the Mosel valley in Germany, fine and not unlike a hock; comes in the same shape bottle as the hock, but instead of being brown, its glass is green.

# Mould
A receptacle to hold a mixture in a certain shape while it sets, or is baked. Of the infinite number of possible shapes, some of the most common are:
*Bombe* For making ices. Used to be of copper with a tight lid so that it could be buried with its contents in salted ice.
*Border* Plain ring, flat on top for setting vegetables, etc., in a jelly or cream.
*Charlotte* Round mould, 3–4 in deep, with sides sloping slightly so that they may be lined with sponge fingers. See **Charlotte.**
*Cornet* Conical, horn-shaped

individual mould, usually in metal, around which pastry cases can be baked to hold sweet or savoury fillings, or on which slices of ham, etc., may be shaped to take a savoury filling. Cornets of paper are used for piping small quantities of cream or icing.

*Dariole* (*Castle pudding*) Plain cylindrical shape for setting individual dishes of, say, prawns in aspic, or for baking or cooking individual dishes.

*Savarin* A ring mould with a rounded top, rather than flat. See also **Savarin.**

*Timbale* A high border or charlotte shape for meat or fish creams; if made with a tube in the centre is a tube mould. (A dish served *en timbale* is one piled up in a circle.)

## Moussaka

A dish from Turkey featuring spiced mutton, aubergines and tomato with cheese sauce.

## Mousse

A sweet mousse is made with whole eggs and extra yolks beaten with sugar and cream, flavoured and frozen or set with gelatine. Savoury mousses are made by enriching fish, meat or cheese with cream and setting with a very small quantity of gelatine if necessary.

## Mousseline

A mousse. However a sauce of eggs and cream is also called mousseline.

## Muesli

Raw rolled oats, raw diced apple, or other fruit, and cream mixed together and served cold, possibly as dessert or as a breakfast dish. (Swiss origin.)

## Muffin

A teacake made of the same yeast batter as crumpets, but browned on both sides and thicker. The mixture is poured into metal muffin rings set on a baking sheet, and then baked until set and risen. They are then turned upside-down to brown the other side of the muffin. Muffins are served hot, pulled apart rather than cut, and buttered thickly.

## Mulberry

The large, deep purple blackberry-like fruit of the mulberry tree (*Morus nigra*), whose leaves are used to feed silkworms. Mulberries have a sweet-acid flavour, make a good compote or syrup, but are not grown or sold commercially in Britain.

## Mullet

1. Grey mullet is a medium-sized fish weighing 3–6 lb with firm white flesh and silvery skin like a bass. Throughout the summer it appears in shoals off the coast of Cornwall; cooked like cod or haddock.

2. Red mullet is a much smaller fish which gets its name from its pink, rosy skin. It has a distinctive short barb under the lower jaw. In season from May to September. Sometimes called the 'woodcock of the sea', as the liver is sometimes left in the fish after cleaning through the gills.

## Mulligatawny

A soup with a peppery, curry flavour; served clear or thick.

## Mushroom

(*Agaricus campester* or *Psalliota campestris*)

**(common or field mushroom)**
Common mushrooms nowadays are extensively cultivated and comparatively inexpensive, although some are still found wild in late summer and early autumn. Buttons, caps and flats are the three main types of cultivated mushroom. The small, white and firm variety of button mushroom is known as *champignon de Paris;* flats have the best flavour, but are not so good for keeping.

## Mussel
Sometimes called the 'Poor man's oyster', a small salt-water mollusc which is plentiful from September to April. Sold by the pint or quart, eaten cold with vinegar after being lightly boiled, or in a soup-stew like *moules marinières,* or as a garnish.

## Mustard
In Britain mustard is sold as a fine, dry flour ground from the seed of *Sinapis alba,* a plant of the *Brassica* family. The seed itself is used as a spice in pickling; the name mustard comes from the fact that the seeds were boiled in a 'must' (vinegar). In France mustard is sold as a paste, often with herbs added.

## Mustard (salad)
Mustard seeds will sprout quickly in a warm atmosphere if planted in light soil, or on damp flannel. Commercially they are sown in small punnets and these are sold for the first sproutings which are used as salad. See also **Cress.**

## Mutton
Sheep more than eight months old. See **Lamb.** If mutton is properly cooked it is delicious.

## Nasturtium
(*Tropaeolum*)
The seeds of the common or garden nasturtium plant are hot and peppery, and the leaves and flowers taste like watercress; all can be used in salads. When pickled the seeds can be used instead of capers.

## Navarin
The name given to a brown stew made of mutton or lamb, with root vegetables, by the French Chef Carême in 1830. See also **Haricot.**

## Neapolitan ice

Ice cream or fruit ice, usually of several different coloured layers, set in a plain, brick-shaped mould.

## Nectarine

A variety of peach but smaller and with a smooth skin, almost like that of a plum, instead of the plush skin of the ordinary peach. Grown under glass for later summer in Britain and has a deliciously fragrant and melting flesh.

## Needles

In advanced cookery, steel needles ranging from 5 to 8 in long are used for trussing and larding. The former have a large eye to carry the string used for trussing or sewing up birds or joints after stuffing. The latter taper in thickness with a special end to hold the lardons which have to be threaded through the meat.

## Nesselrode pudding

A cold sweet based on ice cream, with maraschino flavouring, dried fruits and chestnut purée frozen in a plain, tall mould and served with a decoration of marrons glacés. Not very fashionable now; said to have been named after a famous Russian, Count Nesselrode.

## Nettle

This common weed makes a pleasant vegetable if picked in March or early April while its shoots are young and tender, and cooked like spinach. It is also used in brewing a home-made 'beer'.

## Niçois

Dishes made up with vege-tables, fish, etc., common to the district round Nice, in the south of France. Garlic, tomatoes, olive oil, black olives and anchovies are usually found in food cooked à la niçoise.

## Noisette

Containing hazelnuts or their flavour. Also denotes a certain cut of meat, for instance noisettes of lamb, or 'nuts' of the meat rolled and cut without the bone. See **Beurre Noisette.**

## Nonpareil

Nowadays more often called 'hundreds and thousands', these tiny multi-coloured sweets are used mainly for decoration. Also a high grade of capers.

## Noodle

A pasta, long and ribbon-shaped, made from the same sort of flour and water mixture, possibly with eggs, as ravioli. Cooked like spaghetti.

## Normandy pippin

A delicacy of bygone days : the whole apple is cored, peeled and dried, then soaked and gently stewed in a lemon-flavoured syrup.

## Nougat

A well-known confectionery of which there are two main types : *White nougat* is made with white of egg and boiled sugar mixed with dried cherries and nuts, and allowed to set in shallow tins before being cut into squares. The town of Montélimar, in France, has given its name to a type of this nougat.
*Almond nougat* (or *Caramel*) is made by stirring browned and chopped almonds into caster

sugar that has been melted to a caramel, then turning it out on to oiled marble to mould it into decorative shapes.

## Noyau
A brandy-based liqueur flavoured with fruit kernels.

## Nut
The name given to tree fruits consisting of a hard shell containing a kernel, such as almond, chestnut, coconut, filbert, hazelnut, walnut, and others.

## Nutmeg
After the mace, or covering, has been removed from the fruit of the nutmeg tree, the fruit remaining inside is called a nutmeg. Used finely grated and sparingly because it is pungent. Good in sauces and sweets.

## Oatcake
Made from oatmeal, water and a small quantity of fat for binding, oatcakes are common in Wales, the north of England and Scotland, and are one of the original forms of unleavened bread. In Wales and Scotland the paste is rolled out thinly and cooked in a cool oven, or on a girdle, but in the West Riding of Yorkshire it is thrown on to a heated iron plate and hung up to dry when firm.

## Oatmeal
A meal milled from oats in coarse, medium and fine grades. The first two are used for black and white puddings, haggis and porridge, and the third for scones, oatcakes, etc. Oatmeal ground from Midlothian oats is said to have the best flavour.

## Octopus, Cuttlefish, Squid, Inkfish
All members of the same tentacled fish family and all need long, slow cooking to make them tender; mostly caught in the Mediterranean or Atlantic. Squid, sold fresh in English fishmongers, may be stewed with wine or onions, or, like octopus, cut into rings, cooked until tender, dipped in batter and deep-fried.

## Offal
The edible internal parts of an animal killed for food, including heart, kidneys, lights, liver, melt, oxtail, sweetbreads and tongue.

## Oil
A liquid extracted from vegetable substances such as olives, almonds, groundnuts, corn, or animal sources like cod's liver or whale flesh. It is clear at normal temperatures and is extensively used for salads, sauces and frying. Some oils are deodorised, like that from groundnuts. The best and usually most expensive is olive oil, which has a very fine flavour.

When heating oil for frying it should not be allowed to haze.

## Okra

*(Hibiscus esculentus)*
Sometimes called Ladies' Fingers, a native of Africa and known to have been cooked in Egypt over 2,000 years ago. The plant, with its edible five-sided pods, thrives only in southern climates but fresh okra is available occasionally in Britain. If you buy it fresh, choose clean-looking okra with pods that snap easily, not more than about 3 in long. Used for making soup or stew known as gumbo and good in curry or mixed with sharp tomato sauce.

## Olive

Fruit of the tree of the same name which grows in countries on the Mediterranean from Spain, said to produce the best olives, round to Greece. Before it ripens the olive is green; at this stage it is pickled in brine and may be eaten as a savoury or with an aperitif, either plain or stoned and stuffed with anchovy or pimiento. These also add piquancy to sauces. When ripe the olive is black, aromatic and sweet. Green or black olives are a useful addition to salads. Oil is extracted from the ripe black olive.

## Omelet

A very popular egg dish of which the two main types are the plain, or French, omelet and the fluffy, or soufflé type. Plain omelets are made with whole eggs beaten together and are usually savoury; fluffy ones have the eggs separated and the whites whipped before the yolks are added, and are more suitable for sweet fillings. The secrets of a good omelet are really fresh eggs and butter, a true omelet pan of thick iron or aluminium,

not too large and with curved sides, and fast cooking over quick heat. Fillings are usually added just before the omelet is turned out and served, but in Spanish omelets, cooked and diced vegetables are mixed with the beaten whole eggs before cooking.

## Onion

A bulbous, fleshy root vegetable, gathered from early autumn and at its best from then until late spring, but will keep well for all-year use. One of the most popular flavourings in cookery. The main types in England are:
*English onions* Used for all purposes, dark-brown to pale gold skins, medium to large size, strong flavour.
*Spanish* Larger than the English, but much milder in taste, for boiling and braising.
*Button* or *pickling* Small and brown-skinned, for pickling or garnishes.
*Silver skin* Tiny, with pure white flesh, for pickling, particularly cocktail onions.
*Green* These include spring onions (called scallions in Scotland, Ireland and the United States, but the term may also include **shallots**) and Welsh onions or stone leeks, which are

like spring onions in clusters. In Scotland spring onions are also called syboes.

# Orange

One of the commonest of the citrus fruits, valuable for the vitamin C in its juice, the pectin in its skin and pith, and its completely distinctive flavour. Sweet oranges are imported to Britain from many parts of the world, particularly Israel, Spain and South Africa and mainly during winter and spring, but are available all year round. Bitter oranges, called Seville or bigarade, are imported mainly for flavouring and marmalade. Also members of the same family are mandarin, tangerines, satsumas and clementines, imported briefly during winter.

# Orange-flower water

Mainly used as a flavouring for sponge cakes. An infusion of orange blossom is distilled for this purpose, and usually sold by chemists.

# Oregano

(*Origanum vulgaris*)
Common or wild variety of marjoram.

# Orly

A whole fillet or strip of a white fish like whiting or haddock that is covered with fritter batter, deep fried and served with tomato sauce.

# Osso bucho

Traditional Italian dish in which slices of veal knuckle are cut across the bone and braised in a rich tomato or brown sauce.

# Ox tail

The tail of the animal, technically offal, makes a soup or stew of very rich quality.

# Ox tongue

A tongue comes in the offal category and weighs 3–6 lb. Usually sold salted, to be boiled or braised and served hot or cold. For serving cold the tongue is boiled, skinned and pressed.

# Oyster

A bivalve mollusc in season in Britain from September to April; has a high nutritive value. Most often eaten raw with some seasoning like lemon juice or cayenne pepper, but may also be lightly cooked in sauces or soufflés, or grilled with bacon or a little Parmesan cheese. In England the best known are Whitstable Natives, which are also cultivated on the Cornish and Essex coasts. Among the better-known French varieties are the Belons and the green Marennes.

## Paella

A rice dish with saffron, shell-fish, vegetables and chicken all cooked together with a strong flavouring of garlic and served in the same shallow earthenware or metal dish in which it is cooked. Traditional Spanish.

## Palestine

A soup made with jerusalem artichokes.

## Panada

There are several forms of this basic thickening used with meat, fish or vegetable creams or forcemeats:
**1.** A thick béchamel suce.
**2.** Bread soaked in milk or stock.
**3.** Flour, butter and water made into a paste, like choux.

## Pancake

Flat cake served traditionally on Shrove Tuesday—made by frying a thin batter of flour and eggs in a thick pan to form very thin cakes. Served with lemon and caster sugar, or a savoury filling.

## Papaya

A sweet, easily digestible South American tropical fruit, the juice of which is also used in tenderising meat. See also **Tenderise.**

## Papillote

A case made of paper or foil for cooking *en papillote:* raw food, such as cutlets or small fish, is placed with seasoning on the centre of a piece of buttered greaseproof paper or aluminium foil, which is then folded round the food to preserve the juices while it is baked for 15–20 minutes in a moderate oven. The paper is removed before serving.

## Paprika

Hungarian in origin, paprika is a spicy pepper ground from sweet red peppers or pimientos. Some varieties are milder than others and suit different dishes. See also **Capsicum.**

## Parboil

The process of half cooking, for instance potatoes, by part boiling them, before completing cooking by another means.

## Parkin

A spiced gingerbread baked in a shallow tin and cut into squares when cold. Has a high proportion of oatmeal and is best kept for several days before eating. Traditional Yorkshire.

## Parma ham

Smoked but uncooked ham from Parma served in paper-thin slices with figs or melon, as a starter.

## Parmentier

Denotes a dish containing potato, or garnished with it, for instance *potage Parmentier,* cream of potato soup. Antoine-

Auguste Parmentier, was an 18th century French agronomist who helped establish the potato as a popular vegetable in France.

# Parmesan

A rich, spicy-flavoured cheese, very hard and large, made from skimmed milk in the Parma district of Italy. Is excellent for cooking and a good accompaniment for pasta and soups because it is the only cheese that does not become elastic when heated. Is better bought in the piece and grated as needed; goes perfectly with Gruyère for a mornay sauce or a gratin dish, and traditionally served with pasta and some soups.

# Parsley

(*Carum*)
The most common herb of all, once called the 'herb of health'. Nowadays it is used mostly as a garnish, but it can be made into a good jelly to eat with bread and butter, or a delicious soup. Whole sprigs are used for garnishing fish, stalks used in a bouquet garni.

# Parsnip

Sweet, aromatic winter root vegetable, tapering in shape and creamy white in colour. It is peeled and sliced in fingers or rounds before being boiled, then possibly mashed with butter, or fried.

# Partridge

There are two main varieties of this small game bird, the English, or grey, and French, which is slightly larger and has red legs. The latter is more common, particularly in the eastern counties of England, but the grey partridge is prized for its flavour and when young should be plainly roasted and served with game chips, fried crumbs, strong gravy and bread sauce. The French bird is at its best when more mature. Older birds are better braised or casseroled. See also **Game**.

# Pashka

A Russian Easter speciality: a sweet made of curd cheese, cream, chopped almonds and dried fruit and allowed to set in a special mould.

# Passion fruit

Egg-sized fruit of the granadilla (passion flower) vine, originally South American; small quantities are imported fresh into Britain.

# Pasta

Paste of flour, water and sometimes eggs, Italian in origin and sold dried in a wide range of shapes such as spaghetti, macaroni, tagliatelle, etc. Cooked by gentle simmering in salted water and usually served with a rich sauce.

# Pasteurise

Louis Pasteur invented the process of sterilising milk by heating it to 130–160°F and keeping it at that heat for some time before cooling. This prevents fermentation and helps the milk to keep. See also **Milk**.

# Pastry

Basically pastry consists of flour and fat bound with water, baked or boiled and sweetened or made savoury according to the purpose for which it is to be used. Some of the many types are:
*Flaky pastry* For meat pies,

sausage rolls, etc.
*Hot water crust* For raised pies.
*Puff pastry* For vol-au-vents, bouchées, mille-feuilles, etc.
*Rough puff* As for flaky, also apple dumplings.
*Shortcrust* For flans and fruit pies.
*Suet crust* For steak and kidney pudding, roly-poly.
Some French and continental types:
*Pâte brisée* For savoury flans and pies.
*Pâte sucrée* For tartlets, flans, pâtisseries.
*Pâte frolle* (almond) For gâteaux, flans.

## Pastry cream

Traditional filling for pâtisseries. Made by boiling a mixture of flour, cornflour, egg yolks, milk and sugar and then folding in egg white. Flavoured with chocolate or coffee for éclairs, or with orange, vanilla or other flavour for flans, tartlets, etc. Also known as confectioner's custard and in France as *crème patissière*.

## Pasty
See **Patty**

## Pâte
See **Pastry**

## Pâté
Although the word in French means a pie, it is generally used nowadays for savoury mixtures, principally of chicken, calves' or pigs' livers and other meat, poultry or game, either smooth or coarse in texture. They have no pastry crust and are cooked in a terrine and served cold as a first course, either scooped from the pot with a spoon or cut in slices, with hot toast and butter. They should be well seasoned

and have a proportion of fat, as well as some brandy or sherry, to help them keep.

## Pâtisserie
The name given in France to small pastries and cakes.

## Patty
Flaky, shortcrust or puff pastry made into small pies with various fillings; a bouchée. The name is said to be a corruption of the word pasty. A tartlet mould is sometimes called a patty pan. See also **Turnover.**

## Paupiette
A thin slice of meat or fish spread with a farce, rolled up, tied and cooked. Usually served with a sauce.

## Paysanne
Peasant-fashion. Often braised meat or poultry, with onions, celery, carrots, turnips, etc.

## Pea
There are a number of types of this common vegetable almost all of them requiring the peas to be shelled from the pod before cooking. An exception is the French *mange-tout* variety which, as the name indicates,

is cooked and eaten pod and all. Good peas should fill the pod, not be too old or large, and are traditional accompaniments for spring lamb or roast duck. The marrowfat pea is the best for canning. Fresh peas are usually plain boiled with mint for flavouring and possibly served with a knob of butter. See also **Chick-pea and Split pea.**

# Peach

The English peach, with its whitish, soft and melting flesh, has to be grown either under glass or against a sunny wall in Britain. The other main variety, the Hale, with its firm, deep yellow flesh, generally used for preserving or canning, is imported from the Mediterranean or South Africa. The Hale is larger than the English, but both have the same plush skin with deep pink to red flushes. English peaches are on sale from mid-July to mid-September, the others being available at most times, those from South Africa at Christmas time.

# Peanut

Common name for a groundnut (also called a monkey nut) which has two kernels to a pod-shaped husk, pale brown in colour. The kernels have a pinkish-brown skin and may be eaten with or without the skin, raw or cooked, usually roasted and salted. They have a high oil content and are used for groundnut oil and for peanut butter, which is eaten on buttered bread or toast.

# Pear

There are two main types of pear: dessert and cooking. Of the former, many are grown in England and some are imported from South Africa in early spring and Italy in summer. In good condition eating pears are delicious, but they can easily become 'sleepy', or too ripe, and this condition is not easy to determine until the fruit is opened. Best-known varieties of dessert pear are:

*Williams Pear* (or *William's Bon Chrétien*) Medium size, early maturing (late August and September). Very juicy and sweet white flesh; pink-flushed very smooth skin.

*Conference* Elongated shape, later maturing (October). Fine flavoured flesh of creamy-yellow colour; skin is brownish-green.

*Doyenne de Comice* Large size, late maturing (November and December). Extremely good flavour in its creamy-white flesh; rough brown skin.

*Beurre Hardy* Round pear with firm, white and juicy flesh and a good flavour; smooth, dark-green skin. Mostly imported into Britain. Cooking pears are usually small to medium sized and very hard. There are a number of recipes for cooking them, but they are delicious peeled, halved and cored and poached in a thin syrup with a strip of lemon rind until they assume a rich, brownish-red colour.

# Pearl barley
See **Barley**

# Pease Pudding

Pease pudding is to boiled pork what dumplings are to boiled beef. Soak split peas overnight, drain, boil in a cloth for an hour or two; drain and mash or purée in an electric blender. Beat in butter and egg, tie up in cloth again and boil for last 45 minutes with pork. Turn out of cloth before serving.

## Pecan

A nut, the kernel of which is not unlike that of a walnut. It grows on hickory trees in the southern and western states of North America.

## Pectin

A natural gum-like substance which is present to some extent in most fruit before it is quite ripe. It is essential to obtain a good set in jams and jellies. For fruits like strawberries, which have little pectin, the necessary addition may be made by stewing citrus fruit pith with the fruit, or by adding commercially prepared pectin.

## Pepper

Black and white peppers are aromatic spices which strengthen food flavours without masking them. The white is less pungent than the black. Both peppers are produced from berries of the pepper plant, a climbing vine native to the East Indies. The ripe berry freed from its skin makes white pepper; black pepper is the whole berry picked before it is ripe. As ground pepper loses its flavour quickly it is better to have a pepper mill and grind peppercorns as needed. White pepper is used when black specks would spoil a dish's appearance. See also **Allspice, Capsicum, Mignonette.**

## Peppermint

The distinctive flavour of a plant of the mint family which is cultivated for its oil. The plant also grows wild.

## Perch

Freshwater fish abounding in British rivers and lakes, but of little value in the kitchen; very boney, white and friable flesh.

## Périgord

A region of France famous for its truffles. *A la périgourdine* means a dish will have truffles in it, and probably *foie gras.*

## Perry

Fermented juice of pears, made into a drink in the same way that apple juice is made into cider.

## Persimmon

A fruit not unlike a tomato in appearance, with a round shape and smooth skin which turns from yellow to red as it ripens. The flesh, however, is a different texture and has a tart taste. Persimmons are eaten raw when ripe, or used in drinks.

## Pestle and mortar

A pestle and mortar, the trade mark of some pharmacies, is used in the kitchen for pounding meat, fish, etc., to make smooth creams, or for grinding and mixing spices. An electric blender nowadays makes the job easier. The mortar, or bowl, is made of metal, marble or stone and the pestle of wood.

## Petite marmite

A strong, chicken-flavoured, semi-clear soup, named after the French earthenware soup pot, or *marmite.*

## Petits fours

Miniature fancy cakes and biscuits of many kinds, served at weddings or garden parties, or with coffee at the end of a meal.

## Pheasant

A game bird of very handsome appearance available from the beginning of October to the end of January. Can be roasted, pot-roasted or casseroled, but care should be taken with cooking to prevent flesh from becoming dry. Pheasants are hung for 5–7 days before being eaten; the hen bird is more succulent and has more flavour than the cock.

## Physalis

See **Cape Gooseberry**

## Piccalilli

Mixed vegetables pickled in mustard sauce.

## Pickle

A high-strength brine solution for pickling or salting meats.

## Pickles

Vegetables such as onion, cucumber, cauliflower, red cabbage, preserved or 'pickled' in spiced vinegar.

## Pie

The term pie denotes meat, game, poultry, or fruit, which is cooked in a pie dish with a covering of pastry. A raised pie is one in which the contents are completely enclosed in crust, for which special moulds are made.

## Pig

The pig has been throughout history, and still remains, probably the most valuable source of everyday meat in many parts of the world. It is specially bred for the table as a porker; or as a bacon pig it provides bacon, gammon and hams, smoked or unsmoked (green). Almost every part of the pig is made use of in some way or other. See also **Pork, Sucking pig.**

## Pigeon

Small bird usually treated as game but which may be killed and sold at any time. Some are bred specially for eating, but wild (or wood) pigeons are also good eating. See also **Squab.**

## Pike

A large freshwater fish. In France it is much sought-after for making quenelles, for which its friable, white flesh is particularly good. Can also be eaten stuffed and roasted.

## Pikelet

Another name for a Scotch pancake, drop scone or girdle cake. Crumpets are sometimes called pikelets.

## Pilau (or Pilaff)

A way of cooking rice, with or without pieces of chicken or other meats: the rice is stewed in a stock, generally with herbs or spices, until the liquid is mostly absorbed and the rice tender.

## Pilchard
Small fish, mostly used for canning, found off the coast of Cornwall; like a small herring.

## Pimiento
Sweet red peppers sold in cans are usually called pimientos; the fresh ones being known as sweet peppers. See also **Allspice** and **Capsicum**.

## Pineapple
A fruit imported from many tropical parts of the world either fresh or in cans. It has a very distinctive shape and flavour. The fresh pineapple is the most delicious, particularly raw, but all varieties may be used in sweets, drinks, ices and jams.

## Pine nut (or Pine kernel)
Very small nut, not unlike an almond in flavour, found on some pine trees.

## Pirozhki
A Russian pastry turnover made from yeast dough like that of a brioche with a savoury filling of meat, fish, vegetables or cheese. Can be either baked or fried. May be a sort of pancake roll with a savoury filling, to be eaten with soup or as part of an hors d'oeuvre.

## Pissaladière
A savoury tart or flan filled with tomatoes and onions, with a garnish of black olives and anchovies. Comes from the Nice district of southern France.

## Pistachio
Pistachio nuts are the small, bright-green kernels of the nut of the pistacia tree (*Pistacia vera*). They are dried like almonds and may be salted; their sweet, slightly aromatic flavour goes well in confectionery, for instance white nougat, and in creams and ices.

## Pith
In a citrus fruit the pith is the white part between the flesh and the coloured rind, or zest, of the fruit and in which the pectin of the fruit is to be found.

## Pithivier
Named after the French town where it originated, a round, flat puff pastry gâteau filled with a rich almond paste.

## Pizza
An Italian dish to be eaten straight from the oven. It consists of a round of a light bread dough as the base; on this traditionally is a covering of mozzarella or Bel Paese cheese, tomatoes and anchovy fillets, the whole being brushed with olive oil before being baked. There are, however, numerous variations on this theme.

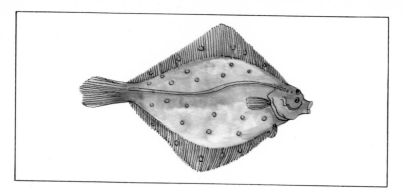

## Plaice

A flat white fish which abounds in European waters and although not the tastiest is very popular in Britain. Medium-sized, creamy-white with a red tinge on the underside, the plaice has a grey-brown back with characteristic orange spots. Cuts very easily into four fillets and is usually fried in batter or egg and breadcrumbs.

## Plantain

Few people know the difference between a plantain and a banana. The plaintain, being bigger and with a more fibrous and firmer flesh, is used for banana fritters, or for baking.

## Pluck

The entrails, heart and lights of an animal which are plucked out (hence the name) after it is slaughtered.

## Plum

(*Prunus domesticus*)
A fruit well-known in Britain both for eating and cooking, ripening in late summer and early autumn. Best-known of the many varieties are :
*Victoria* Oval-shaped, large, with a red and yellow colour, on sale in August. Good for all purposes.

*Early Rivers* Small, red and sweet, on sale late July and early August. Good for jam, bottling or cooking.
*Gage,* or *Yellow* Large, with a yellowish-green colour. Generally used for jam and cooking ; a small 'greengage' plum is used for dessert but is not as good as the real greengage.
*Czar* Large dessert plum with a purple colour and fair flavour. Ripens late.
*Damson* See **Damson**.
*Mirabelle* Not well-known in Britain (but a liqueur is made from it in France), very like the small, bright-red cherry plum ; ripens at end of July and early August and is useful for cooking.

## Poaching

A method of cooking, in a liquid which should be kept at a maximum of 200°F (boiling point of water is 212°F). At this temperature the liquid hardly trembles at all. If water is being used, only small crystal bubbles will be seen on the sides or bottom of the pan.

## Poivrade

White wine or vinegar is reduced and added, with herbs and chopped gherkin, to a *demiglace* sauce, making it a piquant

95

sauce for dishes like steaks, cutlets, brains, liver.

## Polenta
The Italian name for a meal made of maize (corn) which is used in cakes, bread and gnocchi. Semolina is sometimes used as a substitute.

## Polonaise (à la)
A garnish made by frying fresh white breadcrumbs in butter, pouring this over the dish (including the butter), and then sprinkling with a mixture of sieved hard-boiled egg yolks and chopped parsley; the whites of the hard-boiled eggs may also be chopped and added to the garnish. Generally used on asparagus or cauliflower.

## Pomegranate
(*Punica granatum*)
Tart, delicious fruit of the pomegranate tree which grows in North Africa. Has a rough, reddish-brown skin and is filled with a red pulp in which are large seeds. Grenadine syrup is made from the juice, which is also used as a flavouring for jellies and ices.

## Pontac
Boned anchovies and elderberry juice made into a ketchup.

## Poppy seed
The opium poppy (*Papaver somniferum*) has fine grey seeds which bakers sprinkle on some bread and bread rolls before baking.

## Pork
The flesh of a pig, the best being that of a pig which has been specially fattened and fed on milk, although there is a tendency now to leaner and smaller pork joints. A classic pork dish is roast with apple sauce, but pork may also be pickled, or salted, and in this case would be boiled and served with pease pudding. See **Bacon** and **Ham** and appendix.

## Porridge
Once the staple diet of the Scots, a mixture of oatmeal and salted water cooked until creamy. Nowadays it is generally taken as a breakfast food, and new processes of treating oats make it possible to cook them in a few minutes instead of the old method in which the oats had to cook for 45 minutes, possibly in a double saucepan, while being stirred occasionally with a wooden spoon, or spurtle. Outside Scotland porridge is eaten with sugar and milk or cream, but in Scotland it is taken with just a little extra salt and cold milk.

## Port
A fortified dessert wine from the Oporto region of Portugal; used in some dishes such as jugged hare.

## Porterhouse steak
A steak cut from the wing-rib of beef and known in America as a T-bone steak. It should be about $1\frac{1}{2}$ in thick.

## Portugaise (à la)
Denotes that a dish has a strong tomato flavour or content.

## Posset
Once administered for a cough or cold, posset is made by

heating milk and adding ale, wine or treacle, thereby curdling the milk. Should be strained before serving.

## Potato

(*Solanum tuberosum*)
The common potato is a staple food, cheap, easily produced in most countries, and with a high calorie content. First brought to Europe in the 16th century from Latin America. Grows as a tuber; different varieties are suited to different dishes and they range from floury, for mashing, to the waxy varieties that are ideal for salads. Some varieties will keep if stored throughout the winter. They may be cooked in a host of ways including frying, boiling, baking and roasting. **Sweet** (or Spanish) **potatoes** are a tuber of the *Batatas edulis* plant, reddish-brown in colour; usually they are boiled and mashed.

## Potato flour

See **Fécule**

## Pot-au-feu

The name given in France to a dish of boiled beef cooked with root vegetables in a deep marmite (casserole) with water. Unlike its English equivalent, the beef is fresh, not salted; the broth is served as a soup for a first course.

## Pot-herbs

1. Herbs for use in cookery.
2. Mixed sliced root vegetables and herbs sold ready for use in stews or soups in northern England.

## Pot-roasting

A whole joint or bird is put into a deep pan, browned, vegetables and herbs added, the lid put on and the whole simmered gently. It should be basted frequently. Cooking may be completed in a turreen in the oven after browning. Either way is an excellent means of dealing with cheaper meat cuts.

## Poularde

A caponised hen bird. See also **Capon**.

## Poulette

A sauce used with broad beans, veal, and sweetbreads, made by finishing a velouté sauce with an egg liaison, lemon juice and chopped parsley.

## Poultry

The term applies to birds bred specially for the table, such as chicken, duck, turkey, goose, guinea fowl.

## Poussin

See **Chicken**

## Praline

Burnt sugar and almonds in a confection which can be added to soufflés, creams, ices, etc., after being crushed or ground. See also **Nougat**.

## Prawn

A crustacean with long whiskers and horny proboscis, bright red and shiny when cooked. Prawns range in size from the English variety, about 1½ in, up to the 5 in variety found in the Pacific. Best fresh in season, but available frozen (shelled) all the year round. In England prawns are sold fresh by the pint or shelled and frozen by weight.
*Dublin Bay prawns* or *Scampi* are a different crustacean, sim-

ilar to a *langoustine* or baby crawfish, with a hard shell.

## Preserve
Fruit which has been preserved with sugar. See also **Jam.**

## Pretzel
A German savoury biscuit served with beer; has a distinctive loose knot shape.

## Profiterole
A small ball of choux pastry. *Profiteroles au chocolat* are filled with chocolate cream and coated with chocolate sauce.

## Provencale
Style of cooking in the Provence region of France, characterised by the use of garlic, oil and tomatoes.

## Prune
A special type of plum which has been dried and normally needs soaking before stewing. A new drying process has produced a fruit which does not need soaking.

## Ptarmigan
A game bird of the grouse family, hardly ever seen in the shops nowadays. Found on high ground the ptarmigan has brown plumage which changes to white in winter.

## Puchero
Meat, sausages and beans in a stew; a Spanish and Latin American dish.

## Pudding
**1.** A loose term for the sweet course. **2.** Sweets apart from creams and soufflés, particularly steamed or baked puddings, apple fritters, etc. **3.** Meat, such as steak and kidney or steak and oysters, completely enclosed in a suet dough in a pudding basin and steamed or boiled. See also **Black Pudding** and **White Pudding.**

## Pulled bread
Using two forks, pull the crumb from the inside of a loaf while it is still hot, and bake in small pieces in a moderate oven until crisp. Serve with soups.

## Pulse
In culinary language the name for dried vegetables such as peas, lentils, beans. The seeds of pod-bearing plants.

## Pumpernickle
Unbolted rye flour is made into a black bread in the Westphalian region of Germany and eaten buttered or dry with sausage. Imported into Britain very thinly sliced, in packets.

## Pumpkin
An orange-coloured vegetable of the gourd family, with an enormous range of sizes. Can be boiled, mashed, baked, or as a vegetable. Its yellow, slightly sweet flesh is used for pie filling, particularly on Thanksgiving Day in the United States.

## Punch

An alcoholic drink very suitable for parties, which can be made strong or weak according to taste with a mixture of spirits such as rum or whisky. Also contains sugar, lemon or lime, hot or cold water and other ingredients.

## Purée

A thick cream formed by passing cooked meat, vegetable or fruit through a sieve or electric blender, or by beating.

## Purslane

(*Portulaca oleracea*)
A herb not often grown nowadays. An annual plant, the leaves of which can be pickled like nasturtium seeds and the shoots of which are used in salads.

## Quail

A game bird, small and regarded as a luxury; efforts are being made now to restore it to its former popularity and special quail farms have been set up in Britain for this purpose.

## Queen cake

A Victoria sponge mixture baked in small, fancy-shaped tins in the form of various novelties.

## Queen of puddings

A pudding popular in Victorian England: the bottom of a pie dish is lined with strawberry jam and then filled with a mixture of milk, egg yolks and breadcrumbs. When this has set in the oven it is topped with meringue made from the egg whites and crisped in the oven.

## Quenelle

Fish, chicken or veal forcemeat bound with eggs and made into a sort of dumpling; poached in boiling water after being shaped in special moulds or spoons, but traditionally should be oval. Served with a cream or velouté sauce.

## Quiche

A savoury shortcrust flan filled with crisp bacon, onion and egg custard.

## Quince

A large, almost pear-shaped fruit with an exotic flavour, but too tart and astringent to eat raw, hence usually used in jellies or conserves. Yellow-gold in colour, with a grey bloom, the fruit mature on the quince tree (*Cydonia vulgaris*) in late September and early October and are rarely grown commercially in Britain.

# Rabbit
Rabbit flesh, soaked in water to remove strong flavours, makes excellent eating; a lemon helps make the flesh whiter. Ostend rabbit, bred specially for eating, is very good and has white flesh like chicken; wild rabbit, which went out of favour because of myxomatosis, is also tasty and still available. Rabbits are in season during the autumn and early winter, but may be bought all year round.

# Radish
The common radish is a small red root with a strong pepper flavour, easily grown in the garden and used in salads or relishes. It may be round or elongated, and is better if grown quickly. Black radish is another type, being a large, black tap root, which may be served raw in slices with aperitifs or included in crudités.

# Ragoût
A meat such as beef, veal, or mutton in a stew which generally is brown, but may also be white.

# Raisins
Large white grapes which have been dried and had their pips removed. Seedless raisins are of a different type and, like sultanas, have no seeds at all. See also **Malaga**.

# Ramekin (or Ramequin)
A small individual ovenproof case, made of glass or china, shaped like a soufflé dish; used for such dishes as cheese ramekins, or individual cheese soufflés, or for savouries.

# Rare
A degree of cooking in grilling steak. Means underdone.

# Rasher
The name given to slices of bacon (or raw ham) cut on a bacon slicing machine which has numbers to denote thickness: 3 and 4 are thin, 7 thick, etc.

# Raspberry
Common soft fruit plentiful in Britain from midsummer to autumn, with distinctive flavour and colour. There are also white raspberries, but these are not as common or tasty. Raspberries are eaten and cooked like strawberries.

# Ratafia
Small, button-sized, almond-flavoured macaroon mainly used with puddings and cream sweets. A liqueur flavoured with almond oil is also called ratafia.

# Ratatouille
Tomatoes, aubergines, courgettes and sweet peppers cut up, fried in olive oil and then stewed gently with garlic until they become a rich, soft mass. Comes from the Provence region of France.

# Ravigote

A sauce made by mixing hard-boiled egg yolk with an oil and vinegar dressing, chopped parsley, tarragon, chervil, capers and chopped gherkins. Served with cold veal, calf's head or fish. Another version, to be served with hot dishes, is made by sharpening a béchamel or velouté sauce with vinegar or lemon juice and adding parsley, tarragon and chervil.

# Ravioli

Small square envelopes of raw pasta enclosing savoury mince, or a mixture of cream cheese and spinach, which are first simmered in stock, then finished off in a rich sauce, usually tomato.

# Réchauffé

Reheated food. Dishes, such as cottage pie, which are made to use up leftovers of cooked meat.

# Red mullet

See **Mullet**

# Reduce

To thicken a gravy or sauce, and thus concentrate its flavour, by boiling away some of the water content.

# Réform

A sauce made by adding a julienne garnish of tongue, egg white, truffle, mushroom and gherkin to a poivrade. A number of dishes take their name from this sauce.

# Refresh

The process of pouring a cup of cold water over foods that have been blanched and drained, either to set the colour of vegetables, or to clean any scum from meat.

# Relevé

See **Remove**

# Rémoulade

A sauce made by adding chopped tarragon, chervil, parsley, chopped gherkins and capers to a mayonnaise. Served with cold meats, fish and eggs.

# Remove or Relevé

A term, no longer used, for the main course of a Victorian or Edwardian dinner which generally consisted of a joint, roasted, braised or boiled, with a vegetable and potatoes. See also **Menu**.

# Render

The process of obtaining dripping from fat, either by putting the fat in a roasting tin in a hot oven, or by boiling it in a small quantity of water.

# Rennet

A substance used for making junket by coagulating milk. It is obtained from the stomach of a sucking calf. Rennet for household purposes can be bought in a supermarket, but a special type for cheesemaking is sold only by dairy supply companies.

## Rhubarb

A common plant in Britain whose leaves are poisonous but whose stalks, simmered in syrup, make an excellent dessert or tart filling. Originally grown for medicinal uses. The best rhubarb is that which has been forced, and is thus thinner and more delicate.

## Rice

The grain of a type of grass which requires a lot of moisture, particularly in the ground, and thus thrives in sub-tropical climates. The main types are:
*Patna* For curries, pilaffs, etc., has a long, thin grain.
*Spanish Jap* or *Java* For milk puddings and risottos, has a short, thick grain.
*Italian* For risottos, large and thick white grains.
*Carolina* For creams, milk puddings, medium thick grain.
*Ground rice* Consists of rice ground to a medium fine powder and generally is used for thickening, and in cakes and puddings.
*Wild rice* Is a different sort of plant, regarded as a luxury and imported into Britain from the United States.

## Ricotta

A curd cheese made in Italy.

## Rillettes

A French dish made by shredding fat and lean pork which has been fried in pork fat with herbs and seasoning, then pounding it into a paste. Generally made in earthenware pots and eaten cold, like a pâté, with bread and butter. *Rillettes de porc* also may be made from the small intestine of the pig, like chitterlings.

## Risotto

A rice dish, popular in Italy, of which there are numerous forms depending on what is added; the dish is always finished off with cheese. *Risotto milanese,* for instance, has bone marrow and mushrooms added to the rice, which is cooked by simmering gently in stock; *Risotto napolitana* is made by adding tomatoes.

## Rissole

A dish made with cold cooked meat, which is minced, made into turnovers with flaky pastry, possibly dipped in egg and breadcrumbs, or crushed vermicelli, and deep fried. See also **Croquette.**

## Rissoler

To brown slowly in fat.

## Roast

In elaborate menus the roast is the dish that follows the sorbet and comes before the entremêts. Nowadays it is usually meat, but may also be poultry or game.

# Roasting
A method of cooking food, particularly meat, by radiant heat; to be done properly meat should be roasted on a spit, gas or electric, or over an open fire, and should be basted frequently.

# Robert
A sauce with a piquant flavour to go with pork, steak or kidneys. Made by adding mustard and white wine to a *demi-glace* base.

# Rock salmon
A fish and chip shop favourite, also known as rock eel or cat fish; flesh is firm with a slightly pink tinge.

# Rock salt
See **Salt**

# Röd Gröd
A dessert made in Denmark from red currants or raspberries and sago (sometimes used as a soup). Polish or Russian *Kissel,* a similar dish, has currants and black cherries added to the red fruit and is thickened with arrowroot; can also serve as either sweet or soup.

# Roe
Name given to the reproductive glands of a fish, soft roe or milt in the male or hard roe in the female.

# Roll-mop
A boned herring, rolled round an onion slice, secured with a toothpick and pickled in spiced vinegar.

# Roly-poly
A pudding made in the shape of a Swiss roll with suet crust spread with golden syrup or jam, and either baked or boiled.

# Roquefort
A blue-veined cheese from the small town of the same name in the Aveyron region of France, made from ewe's milk and mouldy breadcrumbs. The limestone caves in which it matures are said to help give it its famous flavour.

# Rosemary
(*Rosmarinus officinalis*)
A bush with aromatic leaves and pale blue flowers. As a culinary herb it should be used in the spray or a few of the needle-like leaves can be stripped from the stem and used whole. A few cooked whole with sauté potatoes give a delicious flavour; or place a spray in the roasting tin when cooking chicken or lamb in the oven.

# Rose-water
An essence obtained from rose leaves, once popular for flavouring creams, sponge cakes, etc., but nowadays mostly used in toilet preparations. Sold by chemists.

# Rouennaise
Pertaining to the Rouen district of France. Rouennaise sauce consists of meat glaze, jellied stock and red wine made into a rich, concentrated gravy. Duck rouennaise, a speciality of the area, is roasted lightly and the blood extracted from the carcass by pressing; this is added to the duck liver, *beurre manié*, stock and red wine to make the sauce.

## Roux

A liaison made with butter and flour and used in velouté, béchamel and brown sauces; liquids will blend more easily with the roux if it is made with more butter than flour.

## Royale

A garnish made by steaming cream with egg yolk (for yellow royale) or egg white (for white royale) until firm, then cutting the resulting custard into strips.

## Rum

A spirit distilled from the by-products of making sugar from cane; mostly imported into Britain from the West Indies.

## Rusk

Bread dough of light texture, fashioned into fingers or other shapes and baked crisp right through. Sold under various trade names. See **Zwieback**.

## Russe (à la)

Russian style, usually denoting sour cream or beetroot or both as ingredients. A salad of apple, potato, beetroot, cucumber and peas mixed with fish or meat and given a coating of mayonnaise is called Russian salad. See also **Charlotte Russe**.

## Rust

The crusty exterior of ham or bacon on the side opposite the rind. This usually has an unpleasantly strong flavour and should be discarded

## Rye

An important cereal akin to barley or wheat, used widely in Continental Europe and other parts of the world but not extensively cultivated in Britain. Mostly used for bread, from the black to lighter varieties, and in production of rye whisky.

## Sabayon

Similar to the Italian dessert zabaglione, this French version uses whole eggs (instead of yolks), white wine (instead of the Italian marsala) with sugar. The ingredients are whisked together over heat to a nice mousse consistency and served either as a sauce to a hot pudding, or as a sweet in its own right served in glasses with sponge fingers or ratafias.

## Sablé

Equal parts of butter and flour made into a rich biscuit paste, either sweetened to go with jam or cheese-flavoured as a savoury.

## Saccharometer

An essential piece of equipment in making some confectionery, *marrons glacés* and water ices, the saccharometer measures the density of sugar in a syrup by its specific gravity.

## Sacristans

Pastry twists made from puff pastry or trimmings, which

should be rolled, folded, dusted with caster sugar instead of flour and chilled. The pastry is then cut into strips $\frac{3}{4}$ in wide and about 6 in long, twisted well, placed on a damp baking sheet and baked until brown in a hot oven. The sugar caramelises and gives a pleasant colour to the pastries.

# Saddle
Lamb (or mutton) cut in such a way that the two loins and connecting vertebrae remain in one piece.

# Saffron
Flavouring and colouring in the stamen of the saffron crocus (*Crocus sativus*). Used in savoury rice dishes, cakes and bread. A little is used—a pinch dissolved in a few tablespoons of warm water is usually enough—and as it is light in weight, saffron is usually sold in very small quantities.

# Sage
(*Salvia officinalis*)
This perennial herb is the one most usually associated with goose, duck or rich meats. Also used for flavouring crab apple or gooseberry jelly, and sage leaves are sometimes wrapped round cheese to give it a flavour.

# Sago
Fashionable as a nourishing invalid food up to the turn of the century, but the theory of its nutritional value was discounted in the early part of this century. Comes from the pith of the palm tree and may be used for thickening, like arrowroot. Used in Scandinavian röd gröd. Can be stewed with

apple and served cold with cream, or simmered in milk until clear, cooled, sweetened and served with whipped cream.

# Saignant
Degree to which meat or game is roasted or grilled: blood should run out when it is cut. Extremely underdone (literally 'bloody'). Used especially of wild duck.

# Saithe
See Coal-Fish

# Salad
The name usually applied to a dish of raw, mixed vegetables, but extended also to cold cooked vegetables, fruit, fish, meat, cereals, eggs and so on, in dishes which may be served separately or as an accompaniment to another dish. The commonest forms are of raw greens like lettuce, chicory, cresses, cucumber and root vegetables. Salad is often served as a side dish with meat, poultry or game; it usually has a dressing, either a French dressing or a mayonnaise, or cream sauce for the more sophisticated dishes.

## Salamander

A long-handled iron plate which was held in the fire until red hot, then held over a dish to brown the surface in the days before gas or electric grills were invented.

## Salambo

A small piece of well-baked choux pastry topped with caramel and filled with orange whipped cream; usually served as a small pastry or petits fours.

## Salami

See **Continental Sausages**

## Sally Lunn

A very light teacake split open and buttered while hot, to be eaten immediately. The name is said to originate from the late 18th century, when Sally Lunn became famous for her home-made tea biscuits, which she sold in the streets of Bath.

## Salmagundi

An 18th century dish with a name that rolls round the tongue: the dish itself sounds equally attractive, being a mixed salad of cold cooked and sliced meats, beetroot, cucumber, hard-boiled eggs, etc.

## Salmis

A type of ragoût, usually of duck or game. The bird is first lightly roasted and, after being jointed or split, is simmered gently in a rich brown sauce containing red wine. Should be served with fried bread croûtons.

## Salmon

This 'king of fish' weighs an average of between 10 and 25 lb when 3 years old or more, the young fish below that age and size which have been down to the sea for the first time being known as 'grilse'. Salmon are partly sea fish but return to the rivers to spawn and are usually caught at the river mouth, the season being roughly from February to August depending on the area. Salmon may be bought fresh, whole or in steaks, or smoked, dried or canned. Fresh salmon is usually poached and served cold with a mayonnaise or tartare sauce, or hot with a hollandaise sauce or anchovy butter.

## Salmon trout
### (or Sea trout)

Resembles a small salmon, with silvery skin and pale pink, delicate flesh, also returning to a river to spawn, but the two fish are no relation. Salmon trout average between $2\frac{1}{2}$ and 6 lb and are in season May to July. They are cooked and served much the same as salmon and nowadays are regarded as more delicate than the salmon, although years ago they were thought to be inferior.

## Salpicon

The name given to a mixture of shredded ham, chicken, game

or mushrooms, bound with a rich sauce, brown or white. May be used as a stuffing for pastry cases and other dishes, or made into croquettes.

## Sal-Prunella
A form of saltpetre used to hasten the process of salting or pickling. Use with care.

## Salsify
There are two varieties of this delicious vegetable, sometimes called the oyster of the garden. Black salsify, or scorzonera, with a long, tapering root, is the more prized because of its delicate flavour. White salsify has a thicker and shorter root. Both should be well cleaned by scrubbing, then scraped or thinly peeled and boiled in salted water with a slice of lemon until tender (about 40 minutes). May be served hot with melted butter, or cold in salad, or coated with egg and crumbs and deep fried.

## Salt
This commonest of kitchen ingredients is the chemical, sodium chloride. For kitchen use it is in rough or block form, but for table use it is refined in a process that ensures that it will pour freely. There are other grades and types of salt such as Rock (or bay) salt, in coarse crystals, or freezing salt. See also **Freezer**.

## Saltpetre
Nitrate of potash used in the process of pickling meats such as beef, tongue, etc., in conjunction with ordinary salt.

## Samphire
A spring plant (May) used as a green salad or for pickling; grows on sea marshes, sand dunes, etc., particularly in East Anglia, and is to be found in shops along the east coast of Britain.

## Sandwich
The story goes that the Earl of Sandwich, too intent on continuing at the gaming table to take a meal, sent for a piece of meat with buttered bread on each side of it and thus invented the sandwich. Nowadays there is an almost infinite variety of sandwich fillings.

## Sangaree
A drink from the West Indies: port, spices, crushed ice, sweetening and a lacing of brandy in a long glass.

## Sardine
The sardine is the young of the pilchard and is netted off the coasts of Portugal, Spain and France. Because they do not travel well they are exported from these areas canned in oil or tomato sauce, or salted, and only relatively few people know the delights of fresh sardines. They are used mostly for hors d'oeuvre or savouries. Their name comes from the fact that they were discovered near Sardinia.

## Satsuma
A Spanish variety of tangerine, imported into England from mid-November and popular because it is particularly juicy and large.

## Sauce
A sauce is a seasoned liquid with or in which food is served. Bottled proprietary sauces like Worcestershire, tomato ketchup,

etc., are condiments. Generally sauces are made by using the cooking liquid from the food with which they are to be served, thickened with, for instance, flour and butter or egg yolks, but there are many ways of arriving at an end result that will accompany, coat or cover a dish or bind its ingredients together. See also **Aioli, Béarnaise, Béchamel, Bercy, Bigarade, Blanche, Bordelaise, Bread Sauce, Brown, Chaudfroid, Demi-Glace, Espagnole, Hollandaise, Mayonnaise, Mornay, Poivrade, Poulette, Ravigote, Reform, Rémoulade, Robert, Rouennaise, Soubise, Suprême, Tartare, Velouté, Vinaigrette.**

## Saucepan

A vessel with a lid and handle which should be $4\frac{1}{2}$–5 in deep so as to allow the contents to be stirred without spilling over the sides while the vessel is on the heat. For sauce, it should be small so that the minimum surface is exposed to the air. A milk saucepan has no lid, has sloping sides and a lip for easy pouring. Saucepans are made of many materials such as aluminium, enamelled iron, tin-lined copper, stainless steel, fireproof glass, etc.

## Sauerkraut

Sour or fermented cabbage. White drumhead cabbage is sliced finely and allowed to ferment in brine for about 4 weeks; usually it can be bought ready for blanching and cooking from delicatessens, or in tins. See also **Blanche.** Braised or stewed, it is used to go with rich meat like goose, boiled

pork and sausages. The French equivalent is *choucroûte* and one of the traditional dishes of the Alsace region is a choucroûte garnie.

## Sausage

Meat and a farce such as breadcrumbs, mixed and finely minced or ground with seasonings and stuffed into a gut casing. There are many sorts, beef and pork (or a mixture of both) being the most popular nowadays. See also **Continental Sausages.** Most commercially made sausages contain preservative, otherwise they deteriorate very quickly.

## Sauté

To brown food in butter, or oil and butter, generally before cooking is completed in a 'small' sauce, one made in the sauté pan on the food. The process is particularly suitable for young or good quality food such as a small chicken, veal, sirloin of beef, or for sweetbreads, kidneys or liver. The pan should be wide so as to accommodate the food and allow reduction of the sauce to take place quickly; or a frying pan with improvised lid (a plate, for instance) would do. When the meat is browned it is taken from the pan and the sauce made and reduced until it is just sufficient to cover the meat when it is put back into the pan. Depending on the sort of dish, the remainder of the cooking may be carried out in the oven or on top of the stove. It should be noted that in using a mixture of oil and butter, the oil goes in first and the butter is added a few minutes later and that some foods, like chicken, take longer to brown.

## Sauté pan

A special pan used to sauté meat or poultry. A wide, shallow pan (not more than about 3–4 in high) with straight sides and a well fitting lid.

## Savarin

A light cake baked in a distinctive savarin mould, a ring mould with a rounded top (as opposed to a flat border mould). The mixture is a rich yeast dough which, when baked, is soaked in a syrup flavoured with rum or kirsch. The centre should be filled according to the dish required, eg. *crème chantilly* for a *Savarin Chantilly,* or with cherries for a *Savarin Montmorency.* See also **Baba.**

## Saveloy

A smallish sausage generally made with ground pork, or the meat of a pig's head, well flavoured with spices and herbs. The sausage is lightly smoked and sold cooked. The best are reputed to come from Italy; the name is thought to be a corruption of *cervelas* (brains) because the original ones were made with pig's brains.

## Savoie

An important gastronomic region of eastern France, mountainous and noted for dairy produce, freshwater fish, game and pâtisserie. *A la savoyarde* denotes that a dish will have eggs, milk, Gruyère cheese and potatoes. Among its famous cakes is *biscuit de Savoie,* a type of sponge.

## Savory

There are two easily cultivated forms of this aromatic herb (*Satureia montana* and *S. hor-*

*tensis*). The first is an annual, summer savory and the second a perennial, winter savory. Is used with broad beans, or in some stuffings, and has a flavour similar to sage but more delicate.

## Savoury

The final course of a dinner menu, something small and piquant designed to clean the palate for the port; welsh rarebit, angels on horseback and cheese soufflé are the most popular.

## Savoy

See **Cabbage**

## Scald

**1.** To plunge into boiling water for easy peeling. **2.** To heat a liquid, eg. milk, to just under boiling point.

## Scallion

See **Onion** and **Shallot**

## Scallop

A very attractive shellfish with a delicate flavour, known in France as coquille St. Jacques. At its best in January and February. When alive scallop shells are tightly closed, but they are usually sold opened, with the flesh and orange-coloured roe, called the tongue, attached to the flat side of the shell. The

deep side can be had from the fishmonger for serving in. If bought closed, the shell can be opened easily by placing in a warm oven for a few minutes. Remove beard and cut flesh and roe from the shell with a sharp knife. There are many ways of cooking scallops: baking, frying, grilling or poaching. Avoid boiling or the flesh will be tough.

## Scalloped
Dishes which are cooked and served in a dish shaped like a scallop shell, for instance a *gratin*. Scallop shaped dishes in china or silver, can be bought for the purpose.

## Scampi
True scampi are Mediterranean prawns, but what is sold as scampi in England nowadays might be Dublin Bay, Pacific or other large prawns. Mostly sold frozen, but if Dublin Bay type prawns are bought fresh, they should be boiled lightly and the shells cracked. Scampi may be cooked and served in many ways.

## Schnitzel
See **Wiener Schnitzel**

## Scone
The original scone was made in Scotland, an 8 in diameter round of dough made with flour and buttermilk, or sour milk, cut into four quarters or farls and baked either in an oven or on a girdle. Nowadays the scone may assume one of a number of shapes and may contain white or brown wheat flour, or oatmeal, potato, barley, sour milk, etc.

## Scorzonera
See **Salsify**

## Scotch woodcock
A savoury consisting of hot buttered toast spread with anchovy paste and the whole covered with a rich savoury custard. Served hot.

## Sea bream
See **Bream**

## Sea-kale
A very delicately flavoured vegetable, valued as a separate course with a hollandaise sauce or melted butter. Expensive to buy or cultivate, but repays the cost; not often seen in the shops and then only in winter, particularly about Christmas time. Has pencil-thick stems which widen towards the root, white with a grey-green tip. To cook sea-kale: trim away the roots and tie in bundles, boil gently for 16–20 minutes in salted water until just tender, then drain and serve on a folded napkin with melted butter or with hollandaise sauce. See also **Chard**.

## Sea trout
See **Salmon Trout**

# Semolina

A form of grain usually used in soufflés, moulds, puddings, etc., or sometimes in place of maize meal (*polenta*) in gnocchi, or in bread. It is really grains of wheat left over after a sifting process called bolting.

# Sesame seed

Seeds of the sesame plant, small and brown; much used in the Middle East for a sweetmeat called *halva* and to extract sesame seed oil for cooking.

# Shad

A medium-sized fish averaging up to 10 lb weight which, like the salmon, lives in salt water but migrates to rivers and lakes to spawn. Better known in Continental Europe and America than in England; has a reddish-silver skin and is very bony, but the flesh is highly esteemed. Shad roe is a delicacy. A traditional American dish is shad split, laid on a pinewood shingle and cooked with the wood burning slowly round it.

# Shaddock

The original name for grapefruit, sometimes called pomeloes, which were introduced into the West Indies from China by a Captain Shaddock.

# Shallot

Small, reddish-brown skinned onion with a slightly purple flesh, delicate flavour and economical size for kitchen use. Sometimes called scallions in the north of England. Shallots multiply into four bulbs about $\frac{1}{2}$ oz each when planted. Can be cooked in a variety of ways, or used for garnishes, vegetables, pickles, etc.

# Shashlik

See **Kebab**

# Sherbet

A Middle East iced drink flavoured with flowers and fruits including violets, rose petals, etc., and frozen semi-solid. The name is also given to a variety of water ice in the United States and a children's sweet in Britain.

# Sherry

A wine from the Jerez region of Spain, fortified by the addition of brandy at a certain stage of fermentation. It is a blend of a number of different years' harvests, and thus there can be no vintage sherry. Good sherries are produced in some other countries like South Africa, Australia, etc., but in Britain these must be strictly labelled as such.

# Shortbread

A shortcake baked for New Year and other festive occasions in Scotland. It is made from an equal quantity of butter and flour, very well sweetened and made into various shapes with moulds before being baked. Can be decorated with comfits or candied peel before baking.

# Shortening

A lard or vegetable fat which, unlike butter, contains no liquid and hence gives a very 'short' or crisp texture when rubbed into flour for baking.

# Shrewsbury cake

Somewhat like rich shortbread.

# Shrimp

Shrimp and young prawn are similar in appearance, but a true shrimp has a brown shell and the young prawn a pink colour with a horny protuberance in the front of the head. The shrimp has a better texture and more delicate flavour; may be bought fresh, usually shelled, or potted. See also **Prawn.**

## Shrub
A 19th century drink made with brandy or rum and a syrup and fruit juice. The name is thought to be a corruption of sherbet.

## Sieve
In the modern kitchen a nylon or metal mesh replaces the old fashioned hair sieve, and may be coarse or fine as required; used mainly for making purées from raw or cooked foods. A proprietary type, well-known and useful because the mesh can be altered by changing a base plate, is called a Moulisieve. See also **Strainer.**

## Sild
Another name for brisling, or the young of herring. In Britain they are sold canned or smoked.

## Simmer
Method of cooking food in a sauce or liquid that is kept slightly below boiling point, where the surface is not subject to violent movement.

## Simnel
A mid-Lenten cake usually baked in Lancashire for Mothering Sunday but also associated with Easter. It is a rich fruit cake sandwiched and decorated with marzipan and iced.

## Sippets
Crisp toast cut into small triangular pieces and arranged round a dish of mince, with which they make a pleasant contrast.

## Skate
A very ugly fish caught off the Cornish coast, but with wings or side pieces which make excellent eating, often after the fish has been hung in the sun for several days. Apart from these, only the liver of the fish is eaten. The wings, generally sold skinned, are cut into thick fingers through the semi-gristle or bones and fried in batter or poached. In France *raie au beurre noir,* or skate with a black butter sauce, is a popular dish.

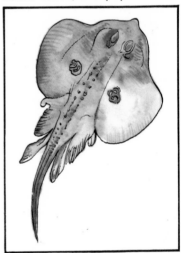

## Skewer
An implement for fastening meat or joints together, or holding meats for grilling. Made of wood or metal, in a variety of shapes and sizes. Some are very thin and round for delicate meats like kidney, others may have an edge to stop meat slipping round in kebabs, brochettes, etc. See also **Attelettes.**

## Skillet
In America a frying pan is known as a skillet.

# Skim
See Dépouiller

# Slake
To mix a small quantity of cold water with cornflour or arrowroot before it is added to another liquid as thickening. The proportion of water to arrowroot is about two tablespoons of water to a heaped tablespoon of arrowroot.

# Slaw
See **Cole Slaw**

# Sloe
A fruit not unlike a damson but smaller and sourer. Used in making sloe gin and sometimes mixed with elderberries to give extra pectin and flavour to jelly. Comes from the blackthorn bush, which grows wild in hedges, and ripens in September.

# Smelt
Small almost translucent fish 5–6 in long, usually fried or baked, served with butter and lemon. Has a distinct smell and taste of cucumber, hence is known as the cucumber of the sea. Popular before World War II, but rarely seen nowadays.

# Smörgasbord
Scandinavian open sandwiches, usually laid out on a table with many different toppings ranging from fish or meat to combinations of fruit. May consist of only a few sandwiches or be virtually a complete meal.

# Snail
Snails for the table come from France, the best being from the Burgundy region, where they are fed on vine leaves. Although they can be bought fresh or tinned in some shops, snails are difficult to prepare and are best served by restaurant chefs who are familiar with the dish. In French, called *escargots.*

# Snipe
A game bird not unlike a woodcock, small but highly prized. Snipe are plucked but not drawn, the head left on, trussed with the legs crossed and the beak pushed through the thighs. Can be spit-roasted, or cooked for 3 minutes each side in a Dutch oven or 6 minutes on a grid in a roasting tin in a very hot oven. Served in their own juice on toast with game chips.

# Socle
A now outdated means of making mounts for dishes in an elaborate cold table by moulding cooked, pounded rice into required shape and then covering with silver paper.

# Soda (Bicarbonate)
A raising agent generally used for fruit, dripping or ginger cakes because it keeps cakes more moist than baking powder and also has a darkening quality. Used with sour milk in scones and soda breads (cream of tartar is used with sweet milk). A pinch of soda also helps when stewing rhubarb or sour plums, or to keep the colour of or soften green vegetables.

# Sole
Considered the best of the white fish, there are two main varieties, Dover (or black) sole, the most prized and most expensive, and the lemon sole. Both are flat sea-water fish, the Dover sole with a brownish-

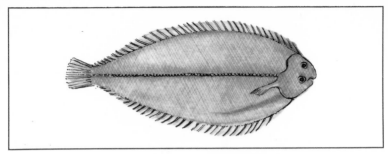

black skin and rather narrow shape and the lemon a paler, more sandy brown and a larger oval in shape. Both are available all year round but are at their best in the months from April to January. Lemon soles weigh 1–2 lb, should be skinned on both sides and can be grilled whole or filleted, fried or poached and served with various sauces. Small 8–10 oz Dover soles called slip soles are cooked similarly. There is a third type, called a witch or Torbay sole, but it is very poor by comparison with the others.

## Sorbet
French, meaning sherbet; a water ice, usually lemon-flavoured, which was served after the entrée in Victorian days to clear the palate for the roast. See **Menu**. Nowadays it appears as a separate course only in formal dinners, otherwise it is served as a sweet.

## Sorrel
A herb popular among European cooks but little used in Britain. Has a fresh, acidy taste which goes well in a purée served with rich meats and eggs and traditionally accompanies a fricandeau. *Potage de santé* is a soup made with sorrel and spinach.

## Soubise
A purée of onions, usually mixed with rice, seasoning, butter and cream, or with béchamel sauce instead of rice, for coating.

## Souchet
Virtually an Irish stew made with fish instead of meat.

## Soufflé
An egg dish which can be sweet or savoury, hot or cold; the basic idea is that the eggs must be separated, the yolk being mixed with other ingredients while the whites are whipped to a firm snow and folded into the mixture just before baking. How the whites are whipped is important since they are what makes the soufflé rise. Hot savoury soufflés are usually made with cheese or vegetable purées, bound with a béchamel sauce before beating in the yolks. Hot sweet soufflés are made on a pastry cream base. All are baked in the oven in a special ovenproof dish or case with a paper band tied round it and several inches above the sides, since a good soufflé should rise a couple of inches above the dish. Cold sweet soufflés have milk and cream as well as eggs, and are set with gelatine.

## Soup
Basically a flavoured liquid eaten (soup is eaten, not drunk) before solid foods to stimulate

the gastric juices. The range of soups is enormous; a clear, double-distilled broth or consommé is probably the most concentrated and best form. This is followed by the bisque, or fish cream, which needs some skill to make. Then comes purée of vegetable, followed by cream soups and broths. The last-named require long simmering of meat bones with vegetables and cereal to give them body and flavour. A broth may also be made with fish. Some soups are really a meal in themselves.

## Souse
A process, used mainly for fish (soused herring) or calf's head, whereby the food is steeped and cooked in a vinegar or wine marinade.

## Soya
The soya bean is extremely useful, being high in protein content. It is the source of soy sauce, much used in Chinese cookery and the basis of Worcestershire sauce, as well as soy or soya flour. The latter is a good source of protein and was used during World War II to increase the protein content of sausages and to make bread. Food scientists are now developing new protein foods based on soya flour.

## Spaghetti
The most common of the Italian pastas, usually made in thin rods about 12–18 in in length; like other pastas it should be simmered gently in salted water after being lowered gently into the pan to avoid breaking its length. Cooking takes about 12 minutes, until it can be broken easily with the thumb nail. Spaghetti should be drained

and tossed with a knob of butter before being served with a savoury sauce.

## Spanish potato
See **Potato**

## Spatchcock
Any small bird which is split down the back, flattened and kept in shape or spitted with skewers, brushed with melted butter and grilled. (An eel treated the same way is called a spitchcock.) Usually served with a devil sauce, gravy and cress.

## Spatula
A flat piece of wood or plastic, like a spoon without a bowl, used for stirring sauces and cream mixtures.

## Spice
The term covering most of the condiments used in cookery, the main ones being allspice, cinnamon, cloves, ginger, mace, nutmeg, and black and white peppercorns. All, like herbs, should be used carefully so as not to spoil the dish by over-flavouring, and care should be taken to see that any particular spice blends correctly with a certain dish.

## Spinach
A common green leaf vegetable which can be used as a vegetable or in creams, soups, etc. Summer spinach is the true spinach (although a winter variety is also grown); it has a delicate flavour and a large, tender, bright green leaf. But also classed as spinach are New Zealand spinach, with a small, dark green and not very tasty leaf, spinach beet or perpetual

spinach (in season all year round) and sea-kale beet, whose leaves serve as spinach. See also **Sea-Kale, Chard.**

# Split pea
A dried pea, split at its natural division. Soaked and made into purées, soups, etc.

# Sprat
Like **Brisling** and **Sild,** the young of herring, about 3 in long, with red round the eyes and a bright silver skin. Usually served either deep fat fried, or grilled, with mustard butter. May also be bought smoked.

# Spurtle
A stick for stirring porridge, still made in Scotland.

# Squab
A pigeon bred specially for the table, killed when plump and young.

# Squash
**1.** A vegetable of the gourd family *Cucurbita,* which may be edible, like a pumpkin, or merely decorative. **2.** A syrup of concentrated fruit juice (lemon, orange, grapefruit, etc.) and sugar, ready to be diluted with water. This generally is prepared commercially and sold in bottles; if made at home tartaric acid should be added to the fruit juice as a preservative.

# Squid
See **Octopus**

# Steak
A slice of meat, fish or gammon, but usually when a steak is mentioned without qualification it is taken to mean a cut of fillet, rump or other beef for grilling or frying, or of chuck or other beef for braising or stewing. See also **Beef.**

# Steaming
Cooking food by moist heat or steam, either in a specially designed two-stage pan, the bottom containing water and the tight-fitting upper part a perforated platform and a lid, or in some improvised form of this. One such improvisation is to place the food in a covered mould or bowl and set this in a pan of water with the water halfway up the sides of the bowl and a lid covering the whole. Whatever the pan, the water in the bottom should boil continually but not violently during the cooking time. Steaming is mainly used for fish, meat creams, puddings and some vegetables.

# Sterlet
A Russian fish, a small species of sturgeon. Its roe is said to provide the finest caviar.

# Stew
One of the basic methods of cooking food by subjecting it to long, slow heat in water or stock; used for meat, fish, poultry, vegetables and fruit. The temperature should not rise above simmering point (190°F). Meat stews may be brown or white, the former usually being of beef browned with vegetables in a little fat before liquid is added and the latter, usually lamb or mutton, being put straight into the water and boiled before vegetables are added.

# Stewpan
A shallow saucepan, often with

double handles to make lifting easier. The handles must be in an ovenproof material for braising. Must have a lid and usually is 3-4 in deep.

## Stilton

One of the best-known English cheeses, semi-hard and blue-veined, although a white Stilton is also made.

## Stock

Stock may be defined broadly as a liquid (or jelly) which has absorbed the soluble parts of meat, fish, bones and vegetables by long and slow simmering. Different stocks are made for different purposes, but the main all-purpose ones are white bone stock, brown bone stock, mixed and vegetable. White stock is made by putting veal bones into a large pan with a quart of water to each pound of bones, bringing to a boil, skimming, then adding quartered carrots, onions, celery, seasoning, a bouquet garni and a few peppercorns and then simmering for 4–5 hours. To make brown bone stock use beef or beef and veal bones, fry in a pan without water for 10 minutes, add vegetables and fry again until browned, then add water and herbs and cook as for white bone stock. Mixed stock consists of just about any trimmings or scraps of meat (but not mutton or lamb), chicken (but not liver), or vegetables (but not turnip), which may be to hand. Vegetable stock is made with vegetables alone (but not turnip). There are special stocks for chicken and fish and one made from sole bones is used for velouté sauce or bisque. The more concentrated a stock, the better it will

be and the longer it will keep, but stock should be reduced by about one-third before being strained and kept in the refrigerator until needed for soups gravies, braises, sauces, etc.

## Strainer

An implement for straining liquids and purées or for sifting dry ingredients. Strainers come in many sizes and shapes from the large Chinese or conical type with a mesh in aluminium, tin or stainless steel, down to the simple small bowl strainer in nylon or wire mesh which can be used for most purposes, including sifting flour, making purées or straining small quantities of stock.

## Strawberry

The luscious red fruit of the strawberry plant of which there are numerous varieties, mostly fruiting in June or July although some types will give one crop in early summer and another as late as the end of October. Delicious raw with cream, or made into jam (added pectin is needed).

## Strudel

Wafer-thin pastry covered with sweet or savoury filling, rolled up and baked in a hot oven. In this country it is usually sold as a sweet. As a savoury the filling may be cooked fish and cauliflower, cabbage and egg, etc. The pastry is of fine flour, water and a little egg, pulled out on a floured cloth. The uncooked dough should be thin enough to read through.

## Stuffing

A mixture, originally intended for flavouring purposes, which is introduced into the natural cavities of poultry, meat or vegetables before cooking. The mixture is minced or chopped, and spiced, generally pork or veal sausage meat, with herbs, rice, breadcrumbs and vegetables. It is also called forcemeat, or farce. When it cannot be cooked with, as for instance with jugged hare, it is fried separately and served with the dish.

## Sturgeon

A fish which, although really Russian, is occasionally caught in Britain. Any sturgeon caught in British waters is traditionally

offered to the monarch and is therefore known as royal sturgeon. It is a sea fish which, like salmon, returns to rivers and lakes to spawn, its roe being the source of caviar. Sturgeon grow as big as 18 ft long, with a long snout and dragon-like appearance and their flesh is more like meat than fish. A few shops in Britain sell smoked sturgeon flesh. Isinglass is produced from the gelatinous bladder of the fish. See also **Sterlet.**

## Succotash

Originally a dish made by the American Indian, a sweetcorn hash or cream sometimes including lima beans, to be served with poultry or meat.

## Sucking pig

A piglet up to the age of about 5 weeks which is cleaned, scalded and stuffed before being roasted whole on festive occasions such as Christmas.

## Suédoise

A fruit, generally a stone fruit like plum or apricot, made into a purée and set in a mould with gelatine; served with custard or cream.

## Suer

The French verb to sweat: in cookery it means the process of sweating meats like chicken or veal, or vegetables, to whiten them and draw out the juices. The meat or diced vegetables are placed in a heavy pan containing a little butter or fat, a piece of buttered greaseproof paper sometimes put on top, the lid tightly closed and the pan placed on a low heat for 10 minutes before other ingredients are added.

# Suet

The non-greasy, dry and firm kidney fat of beef or mutton. Used in pastry and puddings. Now sold shredded and ready for use in packets, but if bought fresh should be cleared of all membranes and chopped finely with a little flour to prevent sticking. Beef suet is the best and can be rendered down for deep-fat frying. In the rendered form it will keep for some time, but to keep fresh suet, old-fashioned cooks used to bury it in the flour bin.

# Sugar

The main sweetening agent used in cooking, generally obtained either from cane or sugar beet, but it can also be extracted from many plants. Main types are:

WHITE SUGAR

*Granulated* Commonest and cheapest form of sugar, used for most purposes. It is sugar refined into coarse granules.
*Lump* A refined sugar which has been compressed into lumps which vary in shape and size in different places; used for the table and very good for preserving or for producing a clear syrup.
*Caster* A finer form of granulated sugar, used for the table, cakes and puddings.
*Icing* A powdered form, for glacé icing or, with egg white, for royal icing for wedding and birthday cakes, etc.

BROWN SUGAR

*Candy* Large crystals, mostly used for coffee, made from string sugar.
*Soft* or *Sand* Consistency of damp sand, pale brown colour, used for cakes.

*Demerara* Useful wherever a sugary crust is needed, on baked ham, bread doughs, etc. Also for table use. Smallish crystals with a honey colour.
*Barbados* Soft, moist, dark-brown sugar, sometimes almost black, for baking soda fruit cakes, ginger cakes, etc.
*Foot* A raw sugar resembling Barbados, but coarser and with a good deal of molasses present in it.

# Sultana

One of the best-known dried fruits, a dried seedless white grape. In its fresh form the grape is small, has a pleasant, slightly acid taste and is usually imported into Britain late in summer.

# Summer pudding

Stewed and sweetened soft fruits such as raspberries, black currants, blackberries, with plenty of juice are placed in a basin lined with pieces of bread, the whole pressed lightly overnight and turned out and served chilled, with cream.

# Sundae

A dish of American origin in which ice cream is served with a nut or fruit sauce in a glass coupe.

# Suprême

**1.** A fillet of chicken flesh removed in one piece from the breast and wing. **2.** A special manner of cooking and presenting a dish, a term used in haute cuisine to denote that only the finest materials have been used. **3.** Sauce suprême is a velouté enriched with eggs and cream.

# Swede

One of the varieties of turnip,

with creamy yellow flesh, firmer, bigger and less watery than ordinary turnips. Cut into manageable-sized pieces and boiled, then seasoned and mashed with butter or served with a cream sauce.

## Sweetbread

An offal, delicate and easily digested, which can be cooked in many ways. There are two sorts, the pancreas and the thymus gland (from the throat), the latter being smaller than the 4–6 in long pancreas and suitable for fricassées or for including in bouchées or vol-au-vent cases. Before being cooked in any way sweetbreads should be soaked for 12 hours or more in water that is lightly salted and changed several times, then blanched with a slice of lemon in the water in which they were soaked. The ducts, any gristly parts and skin are removed, and the sweetbreads are pressed lightly until cold.

## Sweetcorn

See **Indian Corn**

## Sweet and sour

A flavour which, as the name suggests, is both sweet and sharp, and which was imported into Europe with Chinese cookery, which favours it with pork and fish. Usually in the form of a sauce, the sweet being provided by sugar, or honey, the sharp by vinegar and the whole seasoned with a soy sauce.

## Sweet potato

See **Potato**

## Swiss chard

See also **Chard**; a variety of spinach beet.

## Swiss roll

A thin sponge cake which, while still warm, is rolled up round a filling of jam or butter cream.

## Syllabub

A mixture of cream with sherry, or sherry and white wine, flavoured with lemon and served in individual glasses as a dessert.

## Syrup

Sugar dissolved in water; lump or granulated sugar gives the clearest syrup. One pound of sugar dissolved in $\frac{1}{4}$ pint of water makes a good and useful stock syrup. Degrees of sugar boiling, their temperatures and names are given below:

| | |
|---|---|
| 220°F | 'Short thread', for ices, sabayon, butter creams. |
| 230°F | 'Long thread' or 'Feather'. |
| 240°F | 'Soft ball', for fondants and frosting. |
| 325°F | 'Hard crack', for dipping fruit. |
| 380–390°F | 'Caramel', for flavouring sauces. |

400°F and upwards 'Black Jack' or 'Burnt caramel', for colouring, eg. gravy.

## Tabasco
A commercial sauce used mostly with shellfish, etc. Made from hot peppers which are specially matured and treated.

## Tagliatelle
One of the **Pastas,** sold in strips 1–1½ in wide.

## Tahina
A middle East speciality, a paste ground from sesame seeds. Mixed with olive oil and purée of lentils, it is eaten with bread (usually unleavened) as an hors d'oeuvre. Sold in big stores and specialist shops.

## Tamarind
Sweetish but acrid flavoured fruit of the tamarind tree (*Tamarindus indica*), used in some curries, conserves and chutney. The fruit has a dark-brown pulp resembling that of a date but more fibrous. Dried tamarind, or amyli, is imported from India.

## Tammy
A verb meaning to force soup or sauce through a tammy strainer and thus make it very smooth and glossy through emulsification. A tammy strainer nowadays is more usually a very fine double-mesh wire instead of the old-fashioned rough-textured cloth through which the sauce was forced by wringing.

## Tangerine
See **Orange**

## Tapioca
Large granules of starch obtained from the cassava plant which, when raw, have a rough appearance, but which become jelly-like and transparent when simmered in milk. Used in a similar way to sago.

## Tarama
(or **Taramasalata**)
Smoked cod's roe, or grey mullet roe, creamed with olive oil and breadcrumbs soaked in water, sharpened with tomato or lemon juice. This paste is served cold with toast or unleavened bread and is popular as a first course.

## Tarragon
A perennial herb best grown at home if wanted fresh; if buying plants make sure they are the French type with its faint aniseed flavour and grey-green, long, narrow leaves. 'Russian' tarragon is sometimes mistaken for this variety, but has no scent and is rank by comparison. Tarragon goes particularly well with chicken, fish and eggs and is delicate in flavour. Also makes an aromatic vinegar for use in salads, etc.

## Tart and Tartlet
Tart is a pastry case without a lid for holding fruit or savoury fillings, tartlets being the small, or individual, version. See also **Pie** and **Flan**.

## Tartar
See **Cream of Tartar**

## Tartare sauce

A mayonnaise-type cold sauce in which hard-boiled eggs have been incorporated and which is given a distinctive taste with chopped herbs, capers and gherkins. Served with a number of dishes, including fried fish and croquettes.

## Tartaric acid

An acid which can be bought in powder form in the shops but which is also present in some fruits such as pineapple and berries. Used for a variety of purposes in the kitchen, including home-made lemon squash.

## Tea

Tea is the leaf of the shrub *Thea* which is fermented and then dried to give the familiar black tea. If dried without fermentation the result will be green tea. There are many types of both black and green, blended to suit different tastes; all are infused in boiling water for drinking. Much of the world's supply now comes from India and Ceylon. China tea has a milder, more scented flavour than Indian and is best without milk.

## Tea cake

The traditional English tea cake is a large round of bun or yeast bread dough which is baked, split, toasted and served hot, buttered and in individual portions.

## Teal

A small game bird of the duck family, enough for one person. Served roasted with game chips and a salad, either green or orange. May be shot from September 1 to the end of February. See also **Game.**

## Tenderise

There are numerous ways of tenderising meat before it is cooked: steak, for instance, may be beaten with a special hammer to break down the toughening fibres. Mutton and lamb may be treated with yoghourt for several hours before cooking. There are also preparations, such as that made from paw-paw or papaya, for rubbing into meat to make it tender.

## Terrapin

A type of tortoise (not seen in Britain) which is caught in the eastern coastal waters of the U.S.A. Although very much smaller than a turtle, the flesh is similar.

## Terrine

An ovenproof dish with a lid for cooking pâtés or other meats with a minimum of moisture. The term also applies to dishes cooked in this way, like *terrine de foie gras*. The dish should be oval, 6–8 in long, 5 in wide and 4 in deep. To retain the steam the lid should be sealed with luting paste, a mixture of flour and water. See also **Pâté** and **Pot-Roasting.**

# Thermometer

An instrument for measuring temperature, the four main types being:

*Frying* Should register up to about 450–500°F, for testing temperature of fat for frying.

*Oven* Also registering up to 450–500°F for testing oven temperatures for baking and roasting. Modern cookers have a thermometer built in.

*Bottling* Registering up to about boiling point of water, 212°F, for sterilising bottled fruit.

*Sugar* For testing temperatures in sugar boiling. See **Syrup.**

# Thickening

See **Liaison**

# Thyme

A perennial herb, the most commonly used varieties being the black and the lemon. The former has a narrow leaf, the latter a bright green leaf and a decided lemon smell. Thyme is also used in a *bouquet garni* and chopped in all savoury stuffings. It dries well.

# Timbale

See **Mould**

# Tipsy cake

The basis of a tipsy cake is a firm sponge which is soaked in wine, either a white wine or mixture of white wine and sherry. This is decorated with shredded almonds and topped with plenty of whipped cream and a garnish of fruit, either preserved or fresh.

# Tisane

Made in the same way as tea, but using herbs, or fresh or dried leaves or flowers, such as camomile, lime, etc.

# Toad-in-the-hole

Sausages baked in batter.

# Toast

To brown by holding near an open fire or grill. Usually refers to a slice of bread which has been toasted on both sides. *Melba toast* is very thinly sliced bread baked golden brown in the oven.

# Tomato

(*Hycopersicum esculentum*)
A fruit which originated in South America but which is now grown in most parts of the world, including Britain. Although mostly grown under glass in England, the tomato is imported in large quantities and thus is on sale all year round. One of the most important items in cookery, but also extensively eaten raw in salads. There are also purely decorative types of tomato.

# Tongue

The tongue of an animal slaughtered for meat comes into the category of offal. Pig's tongues are usually left in the head for brawn. Ox tongue is the most universally sold, generally salted or pickled, weighing 3–6 lb each. Calf's tongue weighs up to 1 lb and lamb's about 6 oz. See **Ox Tongue.**

123

## Tournedos

A steak from the 'eye' of the fillet of beef. It should be cut thick. A steak smaller in size and from the tail end of the fillet is called a *filet mignon*.

## Treacle

A by-product of the refining of sugar. Molasses, or black treacle, comes from coarse sugar while the lighter and refined sugars give golden syrup.

## Trifle

A dessert which is as English as roast beef and Yorkshire pudding; made by soaking sponge cake in white wine or sherry, covering this with rich custard, jam or fruit, then topping the whole with whipped cream garnished with glacé cherries, angelica and almonds.

## Tripe

An offal: the lining or walls of the stomach of an ox, usually specially cleaned and prepared for cooking by the butcher before being sold.

## Trotter

The term for an animal's foot, generally that of a pig or sheep. The former is very gelatinous; both are prepared for braising or stewing before being sold.

## Trout

One of the finest freshwater fish, weighing between 4 oz and several pounds, caught in lakes, streams and rivers but also extensively bred for the table. Most sold in England is rainbow trout, but there are other types and the colour of their skin, generally a speckled silvery brown, may vary according to where they were caught. The flesh is usually white, although some lake-bred trout are slightly pinkish. See also **Salmon trout.**

## Truffle

A coal-black fungus prized by gourmets for its unique flavour; it grows underground attached to the roots of oak trees. The best are scented out of the ground by trained dogs or pigs in the Perigord region of France after the first autumn frosts. Less good quality truffles are found in southern France, Italy and North Africa. They cannot be cultivated. A truffle may be as big as an apple; they are imported into Britain in tins and are traditionally used in *foie gras;* they also make an excellent garnish or addition to entrées, omelets and stuffings.

## Truss

To tie with string, or secure with skewers, joints, game, poultry, etc., before roasting, so as to make eventual carving easier as well as improve the appearance of the finished dish. See also **Needles.**

# Tunny

Caught mainly in the Mediterranean and off the French Atlantic coast, the tunny is an enormous fish and a member of the mackerel family. Sold only canned in England. Flesh is meaty, firm and white, without a strong fish taste and is very popular in many European countries.

# Turbot

This is one of the finest white fish, flat, with firm white flesh and gelatinous skin. Can grow to an enormous size, but small fish known as chicken turbot and weighing about 6 lb can be bought whole, or filleted, at the fishmonger's. The larger fish are sold in steaks. Sometimes called the 'pheasant of the sea'.

# Turkey

A large bird bred for the table, in the poultry category. Originally American. Norfolk turkeys once were considered to be the finest but nowadays good turkeys are bred in many parts of the world.

# Turmeric

Aromatic, pungent root of the *Circuma longa* plant from Ceylon, used in ground form to colour and flavour curry. Has deep bright yellow colour and, being a dye, is very hard to remove from napkins, tablecloths, etc.

# Turnip

A winter root vegetable with greenish-white skin and pure white flesh, with leafy tops that can be cooked and buttered for a green vegetable when young. The turnip root itself is cooked like a swede; in Scotland mashed turnips are the traditional accompaniment for haggis.

# Turnover

A round of shortcrust or flaky pastry one half of which is filled with meat, meat and vegetable, or fruit and the other side turned over it to make a semi-circular patty or pie. The edges are crimped and the turnover baked like a pie in the oven.

# Turtle

A large amphibious animal which inhabits the beaches and water of south Atlantic and south Pacific regions; is from the same family as the terrapin. The turtle is much prized for its flesh and its eggs, which are laid in the warm sand of the tropical beaches. Turtle soup, a clear consommé with pieces of the green turtle flesh in it, is a traditional feature of City of London banquets. Turtles are neither bred nor imported into Britain and turtle soup is available only in cans.

125

## Vacherin

A sweet made either with round layers of meringue, cream and fresh fruit, or meringue and *crème chantilly*.

## Vanilla

Vanilla pods, about 5 in long, grow on the orchid called *Vanilla aromatica* and contain small black seeds. When the chocolate-brown pod is dried the seeds are easily shelled. Pods give a particularly delicate flavour to custards and creams and can be used several times over. The seeds hold most of the flavour, so it is best to split the pod and extract a few to use with it. Once used, rinse pod in warm water, allow to dry before putting away in a small jar of caster sugar. Sugar thus treated is called vanilla sugar and can be used for flavouring cakes and custards.

## Veal

Calf meat, should have little or no fat and be pink with a greenish tinge. Imported continental veal, particularly from Holland, is usually the best. Veal kidneys make an excellent sauté and the sweetbreads and liver are considered better than from lamb.

## Vegetable marrow
See **Marrow**

## Velouté

One of the basic 'mother' sauces (*sauces mères*): flour is added to melted butter and allowed to cook until pale brown or straw colour before white stock, preferably in jelly form, is added. After being well boiled, and when syrupy, the sauce is finished with a liaison of cream and egg yolk (care must be taken not to boil sauce after liaison is added).

## Venison

The meat of deer, usually red, roe and fallow deer. See **Game**. Venison should be well hung but, with some exceptions, should be cooked before it acquires a 'gamey' taste. Fallow deer is regarded as having the best flavour. Venison can be cooked without marinating, but this will help if the meat is dry. The joints cut from a side of venison are leg, loin, shoulder and best end of neck; the haunch consists of the loin and leg together. Other parts are used only for soup.

## Vermicelli

One of the Italian pastas, used mainly in soups, shaped like a very fine spaghetti.

## Vermouth

A wine apéritif used sometimes in place of white wine, particularly in chicken dishes. After grapes have been pressed for wine, the skins are used in making vermouth.

## Véronique

Means that a dish is made or served with white grapes: eg. *chicken Véronique, sole Véronique* (cooked chicken or fish in a white wine sauce with grapes).

## Vesiga

A gelatinous substance used in Russian cookery, particularly coulibiaca; made by drying the cartilage from the backbone of the sturgeon.

## Vichy

Carrots grown in the Vichy region are renowned in France; the town is also well-known for its medicinal waters.

## Vichyssoise

Chicken stock, cream and leek stems made into a soup and generally served iced. Origin is American.

## Victoria sponge

Cake mixture used for castle puddings, jam sponges, etc., made of equal parts of butter, flour, eggs and sugar.

## Vienna flour

A fine white flour used for special baking purposes such as pastries, rolls and Vienna bread, which is very light and shaped like a long twist or roll. The flour is made by a special process from Italian wheat.

## Vinaigrette

A French dressing with herbs added; for instance, oil, vinegar and seasoning with chopped shallots, parsley, capers, gherkins and vegetables. Served with salads and some meats and fish.

## Vine leaf

In wine-growing countries particularly, vine leaves are used in cookery. Some are cooked and served with strong tomato purée as an hors d'oeuvre; others are wrapped round minced meat and baked, then served with a sauce. See also **Dolmas.**

## Vinegar

The commonest types of vinegar are malt, wine and cider. That made from white or red wine, or cider, is preferred for salad dressings and general cookery while the former, from fermentation of malt, should be used for pickling, bottled sauces and chutneys. A fungus-like vinegar 'plant' put into sweetened water will turn it into a mild vinegar.

## Vodka
A white grain spirit traditionally drunk with zakouska and with caviar in Russia.

## Vol-au-vent
A puff pastry case specially shaped so that, after being baked, the lid can be removed and the centre filled with some sort of chicken, mushroom or shellfish fricassée or other filling and the lid placed in position again. See **Bouchée**.

## Wafer
Extremely thin biscuit in various shapes like cornets, rounded shapes, curled rounds, and of various ingredients.

## Waffle
A flat, crisp cake made by pouring a light batter into a specially made iron with indentations and cooking slowly on both sides over low heat. An electric waffle iron which cooks both sides simultaneously is generally used now. Served with a sweet sauce, especially maple syrup.

## Walnut
One of the commonest nuts used in cookery, grows in a green, smooth outer husk or shell and a hard, slightly rough shell enclosing the inner kernel. Fairly common in Britain, where the green walnuts are often pickled, but is also extensively imported in the shell or shelled from Continental Europe. Used extensively as a decoration (usually whole) or chopped or ground in cakes, biscuits and stuffings.

## Water chestnuts
A Chinese vegetable, much used in Chinese cooking, imported into Britain in cans. Water chestnuts are white, the size of a chestnut and with the texture of a jerusalem artichoke. They are crisp and need no cooking, only slicing and quartering.

## Watercress
(*Nasturtium officinale*)
A pleasant, slightly peppery-flavoured plant which grows or is cultivated in slow-running shallow water in the south of

England and gathered from late spring to the end of November. Used for garnishes, soups, salads, etc. The stalks can be chopped to flavour creamed potatoes, or to go with a herb stuffing.

## Welsh rarebit
Leigh or Lancashire cheese melted with beer in a shallow pan over gentle heat, until creamy, seasoned and spooned over hot buttered toast. For convenience nowadays this is often done under the grill, but the result is really a toasted cheese dish.

## Wensleydale
A Yorkshire cheese of which one variety resembles Stilton, except that its veins are green instead of blue. The other type is plain white and eaten fresh.

## Wheat
One of the commonest cereals, the grain of a grass plant called *Triticum vulgare.* Flour is produced by milling the grain, and the amount of gluten, the albuminous material which abounds in wheat, left in the flour depends on the milling process. Gluten is essential to the fermentation which results in light bread. See also **Flour** and **Semolina.**

## Whelk
Small type of shellfish usually sold cooked by fishmongers or at stalls, to be eaten cold sprinkled with vinegar, with bread and butter.

## Whey
Whey is the liquid drained off from the milk solids, or curd, in making cheese.

## Whisky
One of the best known spirits, distilled in Scotland from malted barley, and in the United States and elsewhere from rye or corn. Rarely used in cookery, although some modern chefs use it with hot lobster and similar dishes.

## Whitebait
The name given to the young of sprat, herring or pilchards found in estuaries round the British coast; fried crisp and deep-brown in deep fat and eaten whole with lemon, bread and butter.

## White pudding
Black pudding without the pig's blood; cooked and eaten the same way.

## Whiting
A type of cod, but small and round with silvery skin. The flesh, delicious if eaten fresh, is friable, white and delicate.

## Whortleberry
See **Bilberry**

## Widgeon
A game bird, a wild duck, smaller than a mallard but bigger than a teal; should be roasted and served in the same way as these two. See also **Wild Duck.**

## Wiener schnitzel
A large and very thin escalope of veal, covered with egg and breadcrumbs and then fried.

## Wild duck
(or **Wildfowl**)
The name covers a variety of wild birds like mallard, teal and widgeon which are classed as game but which, unlike other game, should not be hung for more than about 3 days. Wild duck are best lightly roasted after being well plucked and dressed, make a good **Salmis**, and should not be cooked more than to make the flesh pink. Many people like them saignant; they are usually served with a piquant sauce and an orange salad. See also **Game.**

## Wine
Generally taken to refer to a liquid made from the fermented juice of grapes, but wine can also be made from root vegetables and other fruits. Wine made in Europe, particularly France, is still regarded as best although good wine is made in many parts of the world now where grapes will ripen in the sun. It is important in cookery and contributes subtle flavours to many dishes, and is even more important as an accompaniment to good food.
See **Bordeaux, Burgundy,** **Champagne, Claret, Hock, Moselle, Madeira, Malaga, Marsala, Port, Sherry.**

## Wonder
See **Jersey Wonder**

## Worcestershire sauce
A well-known commercially made sauce used with meats and pies. Made from soy sauce and various spices to give it a very piquant flavour.

## Woodcock
A migratory game bird which visits Britain during October and November while flying from northern Europe to spend the winter in the south. One is usually sufficient for two persons: it is plucked but not drawn, although some chefs remove the intestines and gizzard before roasting and serving on toast, in which the juices collect. See **Snipe** and **Game.**

# Yam

A bulbous tuber, large, with very white flesh and pinkish-coloured skin like a sweet potato. There are many types, but all are cooked like potatoes and imported into Europe from the West Indies, Far East or Latin America.

# Yeast

The oldest known form of leavening or raising agent, yeast is a living plant needing warm and moist conditions in which to grow. Formerly it was bought as a liquid known as barm, or Brewer's Yeast, from a brewer. Nowadays it is bought as German yeast, barm which has been drained and pressed, either as a soft, sweet-smelling cake or in dried and packeted form. When yeast has done its work leavening bread, it is killed by the heat of baking.

# Yoghourt

A non-pasteurised milk which has been treated with a special culture to sour it and make it set. Usually bought commercially prepared, but can be made at home; used as a sweet, also in sauces and dressings and for tenderising meat.

# Yorkshire pudding

Traditional English accompaniment to roast beef; once baked with the meat and served as a separate course, but usually cooked in a separate dish nowadays and served with the meat.

# Zabaglione

A sweet made in Italy by whipping together egg yolks, sugar and Marsala wine; served warm in glasses or cups. See also **Sabayon**.

# Zakouska

An elaborate *hors d'oeuvre* served in Russia (like the *smörgåsbord* in Scandinavia) and with which vodka is usually drunk.

# Zest

Essential oils are contained in the zest, or outer rind, of citrus fruits. Zest is generally taken off by rubbing with a sugar lump, or scraping with a fine grater.

# Zucchini

American and Italian name for a courgette or baby marrow.

# Zwieback

Literally means 'twice-baked'— a form of rusk sold in Germany.

# Appendix

The following pages contain further basic information on cookery including charts on cuts of meat of all kinds, herbs and preparation and carving of poultry.

# Beef

**English cuts**

1. Neck (stew)
2. Top ribs (braise)
3. Rib roast (roast or braise)
4. Wing ribs (roast)
5. Sirloin (roast, or grill as steaks)
6. Rump (grill)
7. Aitchbone (roast or braise)
8. Topside and silverside (roast or braise)
9. Buttock and silverside (boil fresh or salted)
10. Shin and cow heel (stew)
11. Thick flank (stew, braise, boil or press)
12. Thin flank (stew, braise, boil or press)
13. Brisket (boil fresh or salted, or can be pressed)
14. Chuck steak (stew or braise)
15. Shin (stew, gravy or beef tea)
16. Sticking piece (stew)
17. Clod (stew)

# Beef

## Scottish cuts

A  Neck, or sticking piece (stew)

B  Fore-knap bone (stew, gravy or beef tea)

C  Fore-hough (stew, gravy or beef tea)

D  Gullet (stew)

E  Brisket (boil fresh or salted, or stew)

F  Thick runner (stew or braise)

G  Thin runner (stew or braise)

H  Shoulder (braise)

I  Flank (stew, braise, boil or press)

J  Flank – top ribs (roast or boil)

K  Flank – face of (stew, braise, boil or press)

L  Rib roast (roast)

M  Sirloin roast (roast)

N  Pope's eye (roast, or braise)

O  Rump (roast, braise, or grill as steaks)

P  Hind-hough (braise, or boil fresh or salted)

Q  Hind-nap bone (stew)

# Lamb and mutton

## Choice of cuts

A joint which gives a variety of dishes is the **fore-quarter**. This consists of the **scrag, middle** and **best end of neck,** and the **shoulder** which may be cut off and roasted. Or, if this is too large a cut, just buy the whole neck. In both cases, the scrag and middle can be used for Irish stew or Scotch broth, or navarin, and the best end for cutlets or a roast.

Another useful cut is a whole **leg** or **gigot.** Choose one weighing 5-6 lb and divide it into three: fillet or top end, middle cut and knuckle. Roast the fillet end–this may be boned and rolled to make a small joint, and the bone used to make a broth with vegetables. The middle cut can form a sauté, and the knuckle can be pot roasted with tomatoes and onions.

**English cuts**

1  Head (broths)
2  Scrag (stew)
3  Shoulder (roast or braise)
4  Neck – best end, nearest loin (roast whole or grill as cutlets)

– middle neck, nearest scrag (stew)
5  Loin, or saddle (roast or braise)
6  Leg (roast or braise)
7  Breast (stew or braise)

# Carving lamb

## Saddle

There are two ways of carving saddle. In the first, the slices are carved parallel to the backbone; in the second, which is the easier method if the joint is carved in the kitchen, the slices are cut diagonally or at right-angles to the bone.

For the second method, slide the knife down each side of the backbone, then slip it under the meat either side of the bone. Make a cut parallel to the bone about an inch above the dish, and then with the knife held at right-angles, or slightly diagonally to the bone, cut the slices from the bone down the side to the cut line.

Then lift the slices back on to the bone, ready to be served in the dining room.

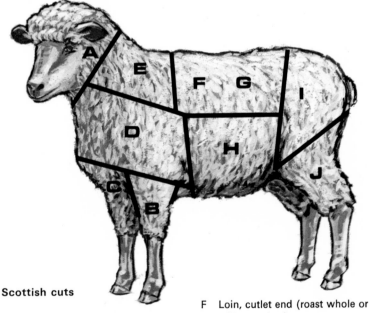

**Scottish cuts**

A Neck (broths or stew)
B Fore-shank (soups)
C Breast (stew, braise or stuff and roast)
D Shoulder, runner cuts (roast)
E Shoulder, back rib cut (braise, boil or stew)
F Loin, cutlet end (roast whole or grill as cutlets)
G Loin, double loin (roast)
H Flank (roast or braise)
I Gigot, chump end (roast, braise or boil)
J Gigot, shank end (roast, braise or boil)

# Pork

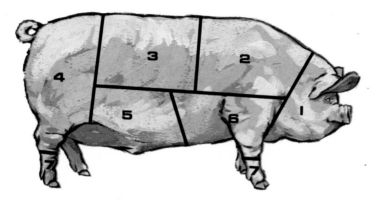

**English cuts**

1 Head (brawn)
2 Neck, or fore loin (roast or braise)
3 Loin (roast, or grill/fry as chops)
4 Leg (roast or boil)
5 Belly and spring (boil fresh or salted)
6 Hand (roast or boil)
7 Trotters (boil or braise)

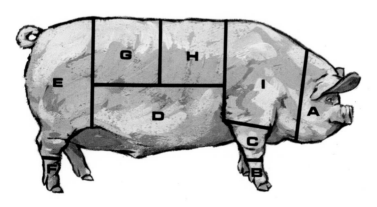

**Scottish cuts**

A Head (brawn)
B, F Trotter (boil or braise)
C Fore-hough (stock)
D Flank (boil fresh or salted)
E Gigot (roast)
G Loin, double loin (roast, or grill/fry as chops)
H Loin, cutlet (roast, or grill/fry as chops)
I Shoulder (roast, or braise)

# Herb chart

|  | BASIL | CHIVES | MARJORAM |
|---|---|---|---|
| **SOUPS** | Tomato & most others |  |  |
| **FISH** | Shrimps, white fish |  | ★ |
| **MEAT (roasts & grills)** | Lamb, pork, veal | Stuffings | Veal, lamb, pork, sausages |
| **STEWS** | Beef |  | ★ |
| **POULTRY & GAME** |  |  | Stuffing for goose |
| **VEGETABLES** | Tomatoes, broad beans | Potatoes | Tomatoes |
| **SALADS & SALAD DRESSINGS** | Green salad, tomato | ★ | ★ |
| **EGG DISHES** | Tomato & fines herbes omelets | Omelets | Omelets ★ |
| **CHEESE DISHES** |  | Cream cheese | Cream cheese, pizza |
| **SAUCES** | For pastas, rice |  |  |
| **OTHER USES** | Tomato dishes |  |  |

We have placed a ★ as well as, or instead of, a specific suggestion to indicate the herb/spice goes well with other items within the categories listed.

| PARSLEY | ROSEMARY | SAGE | THYME | MIXED HERBS |
|---|---|---|---|---|
| ★ | Minestrone ★ | Fish chowder | ★ | |
| ★ | | | Stuffings ★ | If cooked à la meunière |
| Stuffings | Roast lamb ★ | Stuffing for pork | Stuffings | Stuffings |
| | | | (in bouquet garni) ★ | ★ |
| Stuffings (with other herbs | | Stuffing for duck, goose, turkey (with other herbs) | Stuffing for rabbit, chicken (with other herbs) | ★ |
| Potatoes | Sauté potatoes | | Tomatoes | |
| Chopped with other herbs for salads | | | Chopped with other herbs for salads | Green salad, vinaigrette ★ |
| Omelets | | | For stuffing and sprinkling | Omelets ★ |
| | | ★ | Cream cheese ★ | ★ |
| ★ | | | | |
| Maître d'hôtel butter | Herb tea | | | |

# Trussing a chicken

Fold flap of skin over back of neck end, fold ends of wing pinions backwards and under to hold neck skin in position. Place bird on back, press legs down into sides to plump breast. Thread trussing needle with stout thread or string

**1** Insert trussing needle through wing joint nearest you, then through thigh and body to emerge in same position on far side

**2** Re-insert needle into other end of this joint (leaving a stitch showing 1–2 inches long, depending on size of joint) and pass back through body and out at corresponding part of the other wing joint

**3** Tie the two thread ends in a bow

**4** Re-thread needle, insert through skin at end of one drumstick, through gristle at either side of parson's nose, and out through skin of other drumstick end

**5** Re-insert needle in carcass under drumsticks and draw through

**6** Tie the two thread ends firmly at side

(Alternatively use a skewer and string. Push skewer through bird below thigh bone, turn on to its breast. Catch in wing pinions, pass string under ends of skewer and cross pinions over its back. Turn bird over, bring up string to secure drumsticks, and tie it round parson's nose)

# Boning a chicken

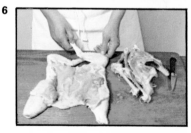

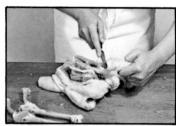

**1** *Remove the trussing string. With a sharp knife, slit the skin down the underside of the bird. Work skin and flesh from the carcass with the knife until the leg joint is reached*
**2** *Nick sinew between ball and socket joint joining thigh bone to carcass; hold end of joint in one hand, and working from inside of leg, cut away flesh. Scrape thigh bone clean*
**3** *Then continue cleaning the drumstick until the whole leg bone is free of flesh. Now remove the leg bone from carcass. Repeat this cleaning process with the other leg*
**4** *Sever the wing joint from the carcass. Still using the knife, work*

*down towards and on to the breastbone; stop there. Free the other wing in the same way*
**5** *Now very carefully cut away the skin from the top of the breastbone. Take great care not to split the skin and to keep both sides of the chicken attached so that it remains in one piece for stuffing*
**6** *Lay the chicken flat ready for stuffing to be spread over cut surfaces. Then sew up or secure with poultry pins/lacers; truss in the usual way (see opposite)*

# Carving a chicken

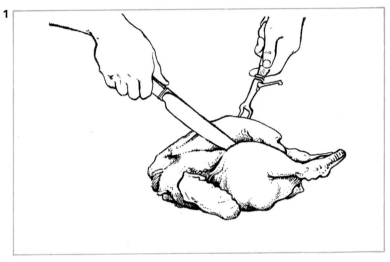

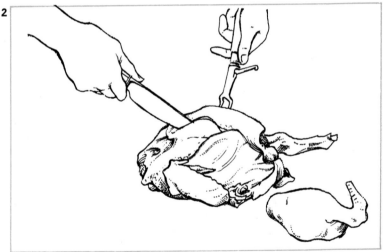

**1** *Hold bird firmly with carving fork through to back, cut skin around leg, place knife between leg and carcass, press gently outwards to expose joint; cut through, slip knife point under back to release the oyster (choice meat on carcass bone) with thigh*

**2** *With knife at top end of breastbone opposite where breast and wishbone meet, cut down parallel to one side of wishbone for a good slice of breast with the wing*

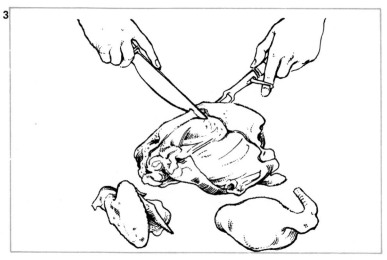

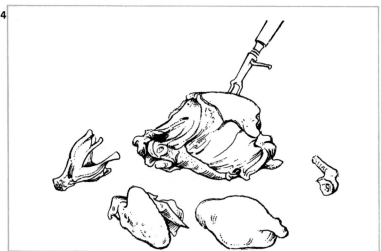

**3 & 4** *Similar pieces are carved from other side of bird. Cut off wishbone by carving behind it down the front of carcass. Carve remaining breast into good slices. (With a large chicken, divide leg into two for good portion of thigh meat with drumstick. Cut through bone with kitchen scissors with half-hole in them)*

# Jointing a chicken

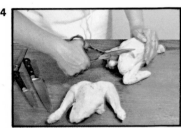

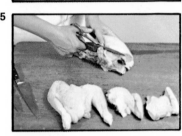

**1** *Hold chicken firmly on board with one hand. With sharp knife, saw away skin between leg and breast. Then, pressing flat of knife against carcass, take leg in other hand and bend it outwards until the oyster bone breaks away from carcass*

**2** *Slide the knife around the leg joint cutting down towards the 'parson's nose', keeping it between the oyster and backbone. Leg is now severed from the carcass and has the oyster bone attached. Cut off the other leg in same way*

**3** *Now make a slantwise cut with knife half-way up the breast across to the top of wishbone from the neck end, to end of the wing joints.*

*With scissors, cut down through wishbone and ribs to detach the wing with a good portion of breast*

**4** *Twist the wing pinion out and tuck it under this breast meat to hold the joint flat. This makes for even browning of the meat. To get both wings of even size, make the slantwise cuts at the same time Detach other wing in the same way*

**5** *Cut away the breast meat in one piece with the scissors. All that is now left of the carcass are the ribs, the backbone and parson's nose*

**6** *The joints are now ready for cooking. The carcass may be cut in half and then sautéd with the chicken joints to give the finished dish additional flavour*